Praise for *Selling is Persuading*

"*Selling is Persuading* is a must read for beginning and seasoned sales persons alike. It organizes clearly the principles of persuasion needed to move a hesitant buyer to conclude a purchase. The strategies suggested draw on psychological understanding, sound economical analysis, and even some cunning. Yakov Grinshpun gives well taken and often entertaining examples that cover the plethora of situations a sales person may encounter. Reading this book can make the difference between losing or completing a sale."

—**Ora Avni,** Professor emeritus, Yale University

"This insightful perspective on the selling process provides helpful hints on the "how to" craft a convincing argument. The suggested approaches incorporate buyers' personalities as well as their representational systems and needs in crafting a convincing persuasion strategy. Great read, highly recommended."

—**Dr. Sofia Velgach,** Industrial/Organizational Psychologist

"In this brilliantly written book on Persuasion, Yakov combines his knowledge of physics with his personal experiences in sales. Starting with Aristotle's quote, "The fool tells me his reasons, and the wise man persuades me with my own," he takes you on a journey illustrating how persuasion is really the basis of a successful sale; one where a buyer is in charge and feels good about buying. Once revealed, Yakov's process of is so natural and makes sense at all levels."

—**Glenn Lippman,** Managing Director, MORE Advantage, Inc., specializing in product development, product brand/marketing and technology management. www.moreadv.com

SELLING
is
PERSUADING

HOW TO SELL YOUR PRODUCTS, IDEAS, AND SKILLS

YAKOV GRINSHPUN

Copyright © 2019 by Yakov Grinshpun

All rights reserved. No part of this publication may be reproduced, distributed, or transmitted in any form or by any means, including photocopying, recording, or other electronic or mechanical methods, without the prior written permission of the publisher, except in the case of brief quotations embodied in critical reviews and certain other noncommercial uses permitted by copyright law.

ISBN: 9781078187237

Book design by Elena Reznikova, DTPerfect.com

For more information visit **sellingispersuading.wordpress.com**

*In memory of Emilia, whom I persuaded once,
and who since then had her way every day.*

Table of Contents

Introduction 1

1. A Salesperson's Job Is Persuasion 7

2. What Is Persuasion? 13

3. Learn Persuasion 23

4. Rapport and Persuasion 49

5. Rules of Persuasion 71

6. Principles of Persuasion 103

7. Tools of Persuasion 121

8. Words of Persuasion 157

9. Strategies and Tactics of Persuasion 189

10. Negotiation Is a Two-Way Persuasion 199

11. Subliminal Persuasion 217

Epilogue 237

Introduction

"*Persuasion is the magic ingredient that will help you to forge ahead in your profession or business and to achieve happy and lasting personal relationship."*

— NAPOLEON HILL

From the outset, it should be understood that persuasion has a central role in modern selling. All selling is persuasion, and vice versa, and salespeople are foremost, persuaders. Products do not move without someone having been persuaded by others or themselves to buy. Our economy would come to a standstill without sales; therefore, persuasion is the engine of the market-driven economy and a key to its success.

Persuasion separates a salesperson from an order taker and is one of the top skills necessary to succeed. There is a direct correlation between the ability to convince others and the level of success and income; especially in sales. But we are all in sales, as the old saying goes, promoting products, services, ideas, and skills. Because most of what we achieve we get through other people, even if we are not in sales per

Selling Is Persuading

se, persuasion skills can get us far in this world so the results we aspire to achieve will come with less effort and greater speed. Arthur Miller in *Death of a Salesman* wrote: *"The only thing you got in this world is what you can sell. And the funny thing is, you're a salesman, and you don't know that."*

The goal of persuasion is, through convincing people, to influence their actions. Influencing is the final step of persuasion.

Among many keys to success, the ability to influence the decision-making process is the master key; nothing is more important to succeed in sales than the ability to change the views of others. To succeed, we are to be so well trained in using every key to unlock the door to the decision-making process we do it automatically.

The information in this book will help to develop the skills that will make the difference between dreaming of success and achieving success, hoping for a better income and having a better income, imagining a victory and winning. These skills are built on the ideas and techniques as old as the Old Testament and on recent advances in psychology, linguistics, and sales.

This book is based on the collective wisdom of many people: great scientists and great marketers through their writings; astute trainers and experienced salespeople through contacts I have made during my twenty five years career as a salesman; and disloyal customers and faithful clients through sometimes painful lessons they taught me.

Introduction

What I have learned from them is that persuasion is not coercion, therefore it requires skills, not pushiness. If we push too hard, we risk being perceived as aggressive, but if we nudge too little, we may be perceived as pests. Persuasion skills allow finding balance that will encourage people to voluntarily move in the desired direction.

The best products and services presented poorly will often be overcome by inferior ones presented convincingly. Yet most salespeople are focused not on developing new persuasion skills but on improving skills they are comfortable with and new technologies as the panacea that can substitute for the ability to influence.

Even with this incredible technology of ours, twenty first century sales need great persuasion skills. It is not either-or. Technology is here not to substitute for the skills, but to enhance them. In and of itself technology does not sell. Yes, new technologies are important, but if we cannot make customers buy us and from us, we shall fail. Technology has not yet replaced persuasion, and probably never will. The proliferation of digital devices helps tremendously with communicating, speeding things up, and marketing. But marketing is not selling.

- Marketing is to create prospects; selling is converting them into customers.
- Marketing brings us to the customers' doors or customers to our doors; selling is what we do when we or they are inside.

Selling Is Persuading

- Marketing is about being remembered, selling is about being bought by convincing prospects to become customers, customers to become clients, and clients to look to us as the best solution to their problems.

For companies like Microsoft or Apple it may be the same. The reputation and marketing efforts of such companies are enough to entice customers to buy from store clerks. But for commissioned salespeople selling cars, real estate, or insurance marketing is not selling. For them, marketing is a very important job of attracting. Selling for them is persuading; that is their main job.

Marketing without sales is dead, and sales without marketing are barely alive.

Realizing that selling, in its essence, is persuasion, I started to research the subject. First I read a lot of popular books on the subject. There are many good books, most covering one aspect of persuasion. While reading, I have discovered that writers are proficient pilferers, so I pilfered liberally. I picked up a little bit from almost every book and applied what I have learned in the field. Some pieces worked, some did not, and yet others needed modification.

It required further research. I read scientific books, attended countless seminars, talked to fellow salespeople, and again tested what I have learned in real life. Everywhere I found useful and brilliant ideas about persuasion. What

Introduction

I could not find is a source that tied it all together. Accepting the best ideas, modifying what I thought to be modified, and adding what to be added, I came up with a system that covers many aspects of persuasion as it relates to sales. I put what I have learned and discovered into this book I hope will be of benefit for people who want to learn basics of persuasion and find the related information in one place.

Persuasion is difficult. While we may be disappointed by the difficulty, mastering persuasion requires time and effort; but it worth it. With persistence and practice, we can develop amazing persuasion skills. This book persuades and motivates people, whose lives and livelihoods depend to a high degree on their ability to win people over, to explore and master the art and science of persuasion. The evolution of selling slowly and relentlessly pushes salespeople toward persuasion. However, there are always those who are not satisfied with the slow progress. They are the ones this book is written for.

Not everyone will become a persuader with a capital "P," but everyone can explore and apply the full array of tools and techniques that great persuaders use. Besides persuasion, the "P" also stands for persistence, passion, and personal development. "P" requires *to persistently and passionately developing our innate ability to persuade.* Performing techniques outlined in this book will greatly increase one's abilities to influence.

What we know may become obsolete, and who we know may become irrelevant with rapid changes in the business

Selling Is Persuading

environment—we cannot count on that knowledge alone. The only thing of which we can be certain is the incessant change, and the set of persuasion skills are transferable into any new situation or career, whatever are the changes.

It is a new world out there. Prepare yourself for it.

Nothing is inexplicable about persuasion. The process appears inexplicable only when people do not know the basics. Because persuasion is the foundation of selling, persuasion skills must and can be learned and mastered. They will intensify your power of persuading beyond its current level. But persuasion does not automatically or inevitably succeed.

If you are independent contractor, imagine the benefits you will enjoy when you master and use the techniques that will help you to lead people. It will make the difference between mediocrity and excellence and give you an advantage over your competition. This book expends your capabilities, opens you to new things, and brings out greater possibilities for you.

Mystery and mastery of persuasion are explained in this book.

CHAPTER 1

A Salesperson's Job Is Persuasion

"Selling is a natural skill. It's developed as a child. You may know it as persuasion."

— JEFFREY GILOMER

Persuasive Presentation

While transitioning from teaching to sales, I discovered that both occupations have a lot in common. In both we talk and listen, provide information and check for understanding, ask questions and answer questions. We can think of a persuader as a teacher, moving people step by step to a solution, helping them appreciate why the advocated position solves the problem best. We think of a teacher as a persuader, convincing students of the importance of learning. But there is also a big difference between them. While teachers provide information and *develop* minds, salespeople persuade and *change* minds.

Selling Is Persuading

Teaching prepares for future actions. Selling makes things happen now.

The main job of salespeople is not to sell their products and services, but to persuade buyers they will solve their problems. After that is done, it will be a piece of cake to sell whatever they offer.

Of all people, salespeople must draw conclusions, make suggestions, and guide customers through the decision-making process. Guiding customers is the very reason salespeople exist. Presenting facts alone does not guide and change minds—reference books are full of facts. The focus should be on altering customers' perceptions of what should be done and convince them to take actions. In today's tough sales environment, deals are being lost because salespeople who just provide information lack the skills to effectively lead customers.

Information Does Not Sell

Salespeople resort to just presenting facts because information hardly ever gets rejected. But it also rarely makes a sale. Customers seldom say *no* to information; the only problem is they say *yes* even less frequently. It is naïve to think that if we provide customers with enough statistics a sale will just happen.

"This family room is 27ft × 22ft." This is presenting information.

Chapter 1: A Salesperson's Job Is Persuasion

"Imagine that in the evening your family gathers in this large family room. There is enough room for collective activities or for each member of the family to comfortably do something individually." This is presenting benefits persuasively.

We may feel in our element when merely presenting facts, but let us try to figure out how much money is lost because of an inability to convince people to follow our advice. It is the ability to convince people to follow us puts us in the business of selling and making money. But money is never spent, at least on our products and services, unless we convince customers to do so. Without this ability, otherwise highly skilled salespeople fail where they should be succeeding. With it, they influence and motivate customers to buy what they are selling.

The following story shows the difference between providing information and persuasion.

A blind beggar wrote on cardboard, "Blind—Please help."

A young man walked by and saw that people were not moved. He asked the permission, took the cardboard, turned it around and re-wrote the sign.

Immediately people began putting money into the cup. When the cup overflowed, the blind man asked a stranger what the sign said. The stranger read, "It's a beautiful day. You can see it, I can't."

Our words not only have to change thinking, but lead to action. People will not do what we suggest just because we think that we can satisfy their needs. If the action is in everyone's interest, it is our responsibility to encourage customers to take action.

Persuasion is not stating our own point. It is about helping customers see why it makes sense to take steps in the direction we recommend. But seeing is not enough, we also have to make them *want* to do that. That is what persuasion is about—to make people want to do as suggested.

It Is Not a Choice

In sales, leading by persuasion is not a choice but a necessary component of success. Whether we succeed or fail is largely a matter of how successful we are at convincing people to buy from us. Technical knowledge is not enough; with the ability to persuade it is what makes sales happen. Persuasion and knowledge breed success.

Successful salespeople are set apart not by intelligence, hard work, or luck, but by the ability to convince customers to do what will benefit them and the salespeople.

To lead people we must:

- Ask questions and listen to the answers. Decide, based on the answers, what we want to say and for what purpose, then say it convincingly, clearly, and correctly.

Chapter 1: A Salesperson's Job Is Persuasion

- Tell, reason, insist, brag, bargain, trade, and empathize to achieve the goal.

We must ask questions, and respond in the way that challenges the status quo and leads customers to see it our way. When used correctly, the ability to change perceptions would get us to our goals faster, the results would be better, and we would have more with less effort.

The effort must begin with the understanding that our customers are not us and cannot be persuaded as if they were us. However, to influence others, we need to understand how we are influenced. Think of a time when someone convinced you and figure out how it happened.

- Was it logic or was it emotional appeal?
- What words talked you into it?
- Were you influenced by what you have to gain or by what you have to lose?
- Were you swayed by the thrill of risk-taking or by maintaining the status-quo?

What works on you is not necessarily what works on your customer, but this knowledge will help you to let go of your tendencies and adapt to those of your customer.

Persuasion is tough. But all people can become skilled in the art and science of leading people if only, besides the technical knowledge of their field, they understand that persuasion is their main job and what is persuasion.

CHAPTER 2

What Is Persuasion?

"I think the power of persuasion would be the greatest superpower of all time."

— JENNY MOLLEN

The Art and Science of Persuasion

Getting customers to see things our way, agree with our ideas, and do what we would like them to do is an art and science of changing beliefs, attitudes, and thoughts. It is an art because personality and style are keys to persuasion. It is a science because it involves principles and rules. Professional selling, persuasion in particular, can be as predictable and consistent as science if it is based on principles and rules. The book of modern persuasion is written in the language of science.

In recent decades researchers made discoveries that allowed transforming the innate talent to persuade, that some people have in abundance and the majority little, into a dependable science available for everyone to maser. Building skills on a scientific foundation, with practice, persuasion can again become an art, the art that gets people to do what we need them to do because *they want* do it. Persuasion now is a practiced art based on a scientific foundation. Influencing others is not magic or luck—it is science. For the lucky few, the art of persuasion comes naturally and effortlessly. Yet for the overwhelming majority, persuasion is a science to be mastered. Persuasion is the "miracle" by which to master selling. If understood and mastered, it could teach us more than selling per se.

Life is Persuading and Selling

Persuasion is not just a selling skill. It is a common misconception that only people involved in sales, marketing, and leadership need good persuasion skills. Everyone can use these skills, no matter their occupation. They are part of our everyday life that permeates every phase of it. Virtually every aspect of our lives involves persuading people (ourselves including) to do what we want to be done, so we can have what we want. Our whole life, from the first cry to the last sigh, we are persuading or being persuaded by parents and siblings, teachers and bosses, spouses and lovers, friends and foes, and salespeople and customers not only in the showrooms and boardrooms, but also in the living rooms, meeting rooms, and bedrooms.

In a day we have to convince a family member or a friend, a coworker or a customer, a boss or a negotiating

Chapter 2: What Is Persuasion?

partner to do or not do something. The essence of life itself is persuasion—how we persuade ourselves, others, and are persuaded by others, how we sell our ideas and skills. Therefore, we are all in the persuasion and selling business. Top notch persuaders will always find employment and succeed.

> "Everyone lives by selling something."
> —ROBERT LOUIS STEVENSON

Virtually every human interaction involves persuasion, but sales and negotiations, particularly, need strong skills to plead our case.

The problem is that many people think that they already have the skills. Everyone understands that to acquire even a minimal level of competence in the field, for example, of physics, one must learn the laws and principles of physics. But most believe that they already understand rules and principles of persuasion simply by interacting and communicating with people in their daily life. Some rudimentary skills they do have, but this belief that by communicating, without a deliberate attempt to persuade, they can achieve what they want, leads people to miss the opportunity to move others and increase the rate of success.

Communicating Is Not Always Persuading

Persuasion requires that we communicate what we want. But it is possible to communicate clearly without getting what we would like.

"This house is well built, located in a good area, and priced correctly." This is clear communication, but is it convincing?

"You wouldn't have to worry about your children too much because the neighborhood is safe and schools are excellent. You wouldn't have to worry too much about maintaining the house because a reputable company built it, and the inspection will show that there are no problems with the house. Because we negotiated a reasonable price, in a few years you will be able to sell the house for a profit and move to a bigger one." Same information, but communicated convincingly.

Although persuasion is communication, communication is not always persuasion. Communication can produce many effects whether intentionally or not. It can inform, teach, and instruct; flatter, entertain, and guide; and persuade, convince, and influence. Persuasion is a motivating form of communication. It is probably the most difficult kind because its goal is to change how people feel, think, and, eventually, act. It does not just happen. We may influence unintentionally, but we persuade intentionally, directing people's thinking.

Persuasion is a Deliberate Act

*Persuasion is a deliberate process of changing attitudes, thoughts, and actions with verbal and nonverbal messages toward a predetermined outcome through **voluntary** compliance.*

The key elements of this definition are:
1. Persuasion involves a deliberate attempt to influence others

Chapter 2: What Is Persuasion?

2. It has a goal
3. It uses words and images
4. People are free to choose

Because persuasion is an intentional act, we have to learn to analyze, organize, and present information so it positions us as professionals who bring expertise, deliver solutions, and offer value to every customer. Communicating persuasively will give us an advantage in motivating customers to buy our products, use our services, and accept our proposals.

- Persuasion is a carefully choreographed dance between the persuader and the persuadee. It is a way to make people understand what we say, believe what we say, accept what we say and, above all, act upon what we say.
- Persuasion is the ability to communicate in a way that makes people feel safe. Basically, it is about customers' beliefs, attitudes, and thoughts. They are set in one direction, we say something, and—lo and behold—they choose to set them in another. Yet easy as it sounds, it is not so simple.
- Persuasion is convincing customers they need it, making them realize that they want it, and showing them they can afford it.
- Persuasion, as it relates to sales, in its simplest form, means allaying customers fears, giving

Selling Is Persuading

them data they need to make informed choices, and making them trust us and act.

There are different ways to make people act. But persuasion differs from other forms of influence such as coercion, bribery, or pressure. It predisposes but does not impose. Although it should influence actions of others, it always gives them the power to choose, (The less choices, the more agreements.) When offering choices, nod subtly when reaching the one you would like people to make. More often than not, they make the desired choice. Dozens of studies with thousands of participants has shown that chances to a positive response to a suggestion are doubled when using the phrase "*but you are free* to choose."

The buyers are asking you to cover part of their closing costs. You are free to say no but would you be willing to consider it?

Usually houses staged sell better and faster. You are free to say no, but would you consider doing some rearranging?

Persuasion is a careful development of a situation where a customer freely makes only one decision, to buy our products and service, the outcome that benefits *all* involved in the transaction. That's what separates persuasion from manipulation.

Persuasion is Not Manipulation

Persuasion is a concept with a clear core and fuzzy edges and, therefore, always raises ethical issues. These issues

Chapter 2: What Is Persuasion?

involve both the intention and the tools we use. Potential benefits of it for sales are immense, but it is open to misuse and abuse. Persuasion is power for good or for bad. It can be either, depending on the objective. If the intent is to find an answer to the question, *"What is good for both—us and the customers?"*—then it is good; if the question is, *"What can I do to win?"*—then it is bad. Use persuasion only for mutual gain, otherwise it becomes manipulation. Manipulation is persuasion gone badly by benefiting only the salesperson. Bad persuasion is called manipulation.

Persuasion and manipulation are so closely related that most their elements are the same; the major difference is the intent. While both know how to convince, the following chart emphasizes the differences.

PERSUADERS	MANIPULATORS
Respect others	Do not respect others
Serve others	Use others
Help others	Help themselves
Work for others	Work for themselves
Create win-win	Create win-loose
Pull	Push
Sell to satisfy needs	Sell regardless of needs

Though manipulation may help make a sale, the sale will never be repeated. In the words of social psychologist Robert Cialdini, *"The systematic use of misleading tactics…ultimately becomes a psychologically and financially damaging process."*

Selling Is Persuading

Persuasion is inducing people to *willingly* and *knowingly* do something that they had not planned. When someone deceives people, they might willingly do as asked, but not knowingly. Manipulation involves distorting and withholding truth. Persuasion implies customers' choice based on trustworthy information and guidance, and is not tricking customers into doing something that does not benefit them. Rather it is a set of principles that allows us to help customers make their own decision from which both, we and they, may benefit.

It becomes manipulative when salespeople distort facts, promise what they cannot deliver, and fail to tell of consequences of taking or not taking actions. Manipulation benefits only the manipulator and is immoral. Nothing is immoral about choosing our tactics, tools, and words to guide customers to take actions to benefit all involved in a transaction.

When persuading, what we communicate need not be false or misleading, but merely presented for the purpose to get the customers to see things our way and perceive us as the best choice to solve their problems. When we alter perceptions, we don't change facts, we just change the meaning by making the important bits bigger and other bits smaller.

For example, we can emphasize our strengths and our competitors' weaknesses, or we can downplay our weaknesses and our competitors' strengths. We make ourselves or our products stand out. It is about presenting us and our

Chapter 2: What Is Persuasion?

case in the best possible light and using the knowledge of human psychology to build rapport, confidence, and trust between us and our customers. If we can find an honest way to frame what we want customers to do that agrees with their needs and wants, our persuasion efforts would succeed. People are swayed until they feel cheated or taken advantage of.

Understanding what persuasion is, we would not confuse it with manipulation. That leaves us only with three methods to make people act without using force. We can order if we have the authority, we can negotiate if we and the other side have to trade, or we can persuade. Command, unless it is hidden, doesn't work in sales. Negotiation, even in a win-win case, is adversarial in nature and is to be a last resort. Therefore, persuasion is a primary and preferred method to cause action. It is non-adversarial and therefore makes customers feel comfortable and satisfied with the outcome. As we progress in our understanding of persuasion, we can modify and enhance our ability to move people.

When we put customers' needs first and then align our needs with theirs, persuasion becomes a bridge between providing excellent service and customers agreeing to pay for it. It is the missing link between the ability to sell and the opportunity to sell.

CHAPTER 3

Learn Persuasion

"The secret is to always let the other man have your way."

— CLAIBORNE PELL

Persuasion Is a Learned Ability

It is the best of times to learn persuasion skills in advance; it is the worst of times to learn when we need them.

In the Internet era when information is free and knowledge is easily accessible, wisdom is still scarce. One of the greatest pitfalls of selling is doing the same things for years. Granted, it is easier to use familiar tools, but it is getting harder and harder even to maintain the level of success you achieved. Ultimately, it is up to people to explore, through reading, attending seminars, and experimenting, what works for them in their field of expertise and master it.

Mastering persuasion is the same as mastering to play piano. Learn, practice, practice, and practice and get results.

Selling Is Persuading

To become a better persuader, invest time, energy, and money into learning the craft. Remember, initially learning is unavoidably difficult. But do not use that discomfort as reason not to learn something new.

What we consider difficult will become normal.

As salespeople, we have to learn as much, if not more, about persuasion as we learn about our products and services. The new reality requires us to acquire a deeper understanding of human nature. It assumes salespeople have enough technical knowledge and skills and concentrates mostly on personal qualities like flexibility, empathy, and persuasiveness.

A question is often asked, "Is it nature or nurture that makes one a master persuader?" This is like asking if the glass is half full or half empty. It is both, they are inseparable.

Some people are inherently talented and just know when to smile, when to nod, or when and how to disagree without being disagreeable. But basically the ability to convince is a learned skill for everybody to master. Whether you have inborn talent for persuasion or not, whether insightful about the methods of persuasion or not, whether a gifted artisan of language or not, it is possible to learn and master scientifically established techniques that allow to be more persuasive. Learning persuasion permits anyone to benefit from it as fully as the born master.

All people learn early in life some techniques allowing them to get what they need. As infants, they have only a

Chapter 3: Learn Persuasion

few ways of communicating their needs. Those ways are loud and for a while succeed. Crying, at first, is a pure physiological reaction to an empty stomach. But infants quickly learn how crying can affect parents. As people mature, through observation and experimentation, they learn additional persuasion skills that work well if they stay in familiar environment.

However, when people have to persuade for a living, they may find that the acquired skills are not enough to succeed. Even the natural ability to persuade alone is not enough to succeed in modern environment.

It is one thing to persuade someone into sharing a drink and quite another into buying something.

Salespeople, who spent a few years in sales, most likely, have good people skills already learned from mistakes they made. And it is most likely they do the persuasion intuitively. If it is not done yet, it is time to put persuasion on scientific foundation and learn to persuade consciously. Contemporary sales require moving from the spontaneous attempts to convince to the *conscious* and *effective* ones.

Learn from mistakes of others who have already figured out everything we need to know and put the information out. Read, learn, and implement.

Those who want to succeed at persuasion, no matter how much or little of a gift they have, need to be:

- Educated, informed, and knowledgeable
- Adaptable, resilient, and cooperative

Selling Is Persuading

- Empathic, friendly, and dependable
- Practicing, practicing, and practicing

Develop and sharpen what inborn power of persuasion you are given. It will allow you working smarter instead of harder. Dull knives work the hardest.

In Stephen Covey's book *7 Habits of Highly Successful People* one habit is called "sharpen the saw." The author tells a story about a young lumberjack challenging the best old one.

They decided that the competition would last for six hours and they would use the same equipment. The young man took twenty-minutes breaks every two hours while his competitor did not.

After the count of the cut wood, to everyone's surprise, the young man was the winner. After he received his trophy, the old man asked him, "What the heck were you doing during those breaks?" The young man answered, "I used the breaks to sharpen my saw."

We always must keep our tools razor sharp. It includes improving still relevant techniques and learning new skills based on recent discoveries, for example, the significant role that the subconscious mind plays in the persuasion process and how language patterns and body language can subliminally manipulate the subconscious. Acquired skills ought to be maintained, refreshed, and expended. Learning never stops. To stop learning is to rest on a plateau while others are reaching new heights. And they may be your competition.

Chapter 3: Learn Persuasion

Our task is:

- To discard that which has to be discarded
- To know that which has to be known
- To do that which has to be done

In the first book ever written on the subject, *The Art of Rhetoric*, Aristotle first introduced persuasion as a learned behavior. Fortunately, unlike intelligence, which is genetically fixed and changes little, persuasion skills are largely learned and change as we learn from our experiences and from studying others. Ineffectiveness at winning customers over stems from a simple inability rather than a lack of talent. Therefore, the solution lies in learning. *"Study the art of persuasion,"* said Donald Trump, *"Practice it. Develop an understanding of its profound value across all aspects of life."*

They say that lawyers can support either side of an argument. This underlines that persuasion is a skill. Like driving, or cooking, or writing it can (and should) be learned. It is possible to master scientifically proven techniques to become more persuasive. It is worth investing time, effort, and, if needed, money into.

These skills are no passing fad. Studies demonstrate that they now make up the biggest part of the ingredients for success. If we are our own bosses as in commissioned sales, our success depends on these skills to a great extent.

To develop the required skills, it is necessary to understand basic concepts and principles, and learn what tools to apply in different situations and with different people.

Different Strokes for Different Folks

1. Misreading people can be fatal, at least to our careers. The following story is a fine illustration of what could happen when misreading the situation.

   A boy walking along the path noticed a struggling scorpion lying on its back.
   "Please help me," pleaded the scorpion, "or I'll surely die."
   "But if I do, you'll surely sting me," replied the boy, "And I'll be the one to die."
   "Oh no," begged the scorpion, "How can I sting someone who saved me?"
   And surely, as the boy turned the scorpion, the scorpion stung him.
   "Why?" asked the boy as he sobbed, "You promised."
   "You knew who I was when you helped me," replied the scorpion hurrying away.

To forecast and manage behavior of the customers we wish to convince, we must first be able to classify them, so we don't find ourselves in the position of the poor boy.

We cannot delve into the world of selling blindly. We have to learn how to read people and charm them, make a

Chapter 3: Learn Persuasion

favorable impression and cajole into acting, remove barriers and eliminate resistance. We must have some insight towards people we hope to convince and know what they think and feel, dream and worry about, like and dislike.

2. If we cannot read and understand people how will we know:

    - How to persuade them?
    - How to change the way they look at their problems?
    - How hard to bargain with the other side without discovering their true needs?
    - What words to use to match the dominant sense they use to process the information?

3. People are different in many regards and usually are not like you.

    - Some do not like surprises; others love to explore the unknown.
    - Some do not mind to make a difficult decision; others need a nudge to make a simple one.
    - Some are task-oriented, others are people-oriented.
    - Some stick to a subject in a conversation; others change it often.
    - Some look for similarities, others look for differences.

Selling Is Persuading

- Some like to keep their options open; others like to pin them down.
- Some stick to what they said; others easily can take their words back.
- Some do not want to be involved; others want to know every detail.
- Some like to see; others like to hear or feel.

This list can go on and on.

If we look for differences, as you can see, we will find plenty of them. But fortunately, if we look for similarities, we will find plenty of them as well. Our ability to see similarities rather than be overwhelmed by differences enables us to classify people according to these similarities. Although unique, everyone falls into a class, a group, or a type. The greatest benefit of classifying people correctly is the relief we feel when we can accurately read and understand people.

There are many ways of classifying people. Some classifications like what month and under what star people were born (astrology) or what year they were born (Chinese calendar) have no scientific or experiential backing. Others are based on our experience and intuition. But the classifications we need to learn are the ones that are well researched by psychologists. Of the latter, *personality typing*, *NLP* and the *hierarchy of needs* are the most important and useful in sales.

Chapter 3: Learn Persuasion

Personality Types

A message that sways one customer may leave another indifferent. Presenting a highly detailed, analytical argument to a customer who actually prefers a big picture can be confusing to them. Confused people tend to say "no." Therefore, we first need to assess a customer's personality type to determine which tools to use. Only in the twentieth century did many professionals recognize the value of understanding human personalities as it relates to their field of expertise.

The ancient Greeks defined four personality types.
1. The Phlegmatic type is calm, steady, and friendly.
2. The Choleric type is impulsive, driven, and dominating.
3. The Melancholic type is moody, cautious, and analytical
4. The Sanguine type is optimistic, animated, and outgoing.

These four types still work well for salespeople. Some scientists now call these four types Amiable, Driven, Analytical, and Expressive, while others use less descriptive names, including those of colors, letters, and numbers.

I prefer self-explanatory names like

- **Belongers** (aka Phlegmatics) are open to us and our messages, but are not quick to decide. Valuing personal relationships, they are great listeners and sincerely want to understand and trust those they do business with. They are friendly, calm, and patient.

    Let them feel understood. Trigger words for Belongers may include reliable, dependable, flexible, and consensus.

- **Achievers** (aka Cholerics) are results-and-bottom-line-oriented and competitive. They may be impatient, especially with lengthy and detailed presentations and want the bottom line presented quickly and logically. Rather than asking questions, they speak in declarative sentences in a louder than average tone.

    Let them feel they are in control. Their trigger words include advantage, return on investment, completed, and objective.

- **Thinkers** (aka Melancholics), because they are detail-oriented, approach the presentation logically and rationally. They want a lot of

Chapter 3: Learn Persuasion

detail and dislike emotional terms and inexact language. They are less expressive than other types, serious, direct, and formal. If arguments support the points we make, they may tolerate a lengthy presentation. Thinkers need and appreciate data, facts, and figures. Like Belongers, they do not decide quickly.

Let them feel they are right. Words that trigger a positive response from them include proven, factual, experience, and principles.

- **Feelers** (aka Sanguines) are people who rely on instinct and intuition. They are opposite to the detail-oriented and do not need too many facts to act. They are creative, outgoing, and spontaneous, easily bored with facts and logic. They love to be involved. Like Belongers, they value personal relationships, but like Achievers, they are sure of themselves and speak in statements rather than questions.

  Let them feel understood and important. You might trigger a positive response from them by using words such as creative, innovative, inspired, and hunches.

Selling Is Persuading

To better understand different types, watch the TV show *Sex and the City*. I liked it not because of the city, not even because of the sex, but because of the masterly portrayal of the four pure personality types. Carrie is a Belonger, Samantha is an Achiever, Miranda is a Thinker, and Charlotte is a Feeler.

In reality, most people will be a mix of these personality types. Attempt to define personality type is akin to defining the color of a chameleon. It depends on many factors. Knowing the basic colors, we can guess its color by observing the environment. Once we are familiar with the core personalities, we should be able to discover customers' personality types by observing them for a while. For all personality types, we must persuade them in certain ways, boost their egos, and leave ours at the door. We must adapt to any personality type, not just to one like our own, and persuade customers the way they prefer, not the way we like to be persuaded.

First we have to understand our own personality type. If we do not, we will understand nobody else's.

Many tools are available for analyzing and categorizing personalities. Familiarize yourself with them. We do not need a detailed picture. We are salespeople, not professional psychologists. The information we need to assess customers' personality types we can pull from commonsense observations which is discussed in Chapter 5.

Chapter 3: Learn Persuasion

To expand your understanding of personality types read *Please Understand Me II* by David Keirsey.

NLP

NLP or Neuro-Linguistic Programming is about how the brain works (Neuro); how the language interacts with the brain (Linguistic); and how to develop the outcomes we want (Programming). It combines neurology, language, and patterns. The neurology part connects external senses like sight, hearing, and feeling with internal representation; the language part teaches how to communicate with others; and the programming part produces the desired outcomes using the external senses as tools.

NLP explains how people process information, communicate, and perceive the world according to which sense is dominant. It teaches how to change perceptions and influence behaviors using different sensory words. NLP made obvious what people already knew intuitively.

"Those that will not hear must be made feel." —German proverb
"The tongue can paint what the eye can't see." —Chinese proverb

For salespeople NLP clarifies their customers' thinking and empowers them to determine the outcome of their communication with customers instead of being just powerless listeners or at best one half of the communication process.

Selling Is Persuading

The theory behind NLP is that how people use words to express their thoughts reflect the way they think. Words are the representation of people's thoughts. When we tailor our words to match theirs, we reduce resistance, raise responsiveness, and intensify rapport.

People tend to choose words which most closely correlate with their way of thinking and are most comfortable in a dialogue with words and phrases that closely match their thinking process. If we can learn the thinking process of a customer, we will know not only the information that customer is seeking, but also how he or she will process and use the information.

Of the five senses, people gravitate toward three dominant ones: sight, hearing, and touching. Accordingly, they are called Visual, Auditory, and Kinesthetic people. As we determine the dominant sensory mode, we speak with different people in "different" languages. So, use words like:

- *Look, overview, focus, image, picture, show, sparkling, gigantic, and teeny-tiny* with Visuals
- *Hear, sound, say, listen, discuss, verbalize, serene, humming, and thundering* with Auditories
- *Tangible, feel, touch, grasp, texture, lift, reach,* firm, smooth, *and* rough with Kinesthetics

In a conversation, we can substitute a neutral word using different sensory words to match customers' thinking patterns: "It certainly seems (*looks, sounds, feels*) like a good idea to me, how does it seem (*look, sound, feel*) to you?" Different customers respond differently to same message presented with different words. Phrases to use:

- I *see* what you mean. From *viewpoint*. Do you *picture* it? How does it *look*? with Visuals
- That *sounds* good. Let's *talk* about it. I *hear* you. Does it *ring* a bell? with Auditories
- I'll be in *touch*. I can *sense* it. I understand how you *feel*. Do you *feel* it? with Kinesthetics

It is not enough for customers to *understand* your language; it has to be said in *their* language.

To determine the dominant sense pay attention to the words people use and to nonverbal clues they send.

Although the underlying science is more complicated, the following technique gives pretty accurate results. Ask customers a question that makes them putting some effort to answer and watch the movement of their eyes. Much more often than not when searching for an answer, if they look:

- Up, they are visual
- To either ear, they are auditory
- Down to the guts, they are kinesthetic

Senses, especially the dominant ones, equal reality.

The Hierarchy of Needs

Customers' decisions to buy are mostly a function of subconscious urges to satisfy their needs and wants. People are always looking for something: love, status, comfort. They spend their lives searching for intangibles. Therefore, leading them involves understanding their *real* needs, wants, and motivations to act. Rather than focusing presentations on services and products, we must concentrate on customers' desires and wishes. As salespeople, our job is to give customers enough information to make a good decision. We do not control customers' process of deciding. We just control the information and the way we present it. At its simplest, our persuasion is a matter of showing customers how what we offer fulfills their needs and wants, and urge them to act. It must be based on the ability to recognize what customers need and want to happen, what they hope will happen, and what they believe should happen. What we think our customers want and what they *really* want are, in most cases, different things.

People's needs and wants are like a tree. What they are talking about is like what we see looking at the tree. We do not see the roots. But the tree is fed by the roots that we do not see. So, the needs people are talking about openly are fed by the hidden motives—their *real* needs. Those often remain hidden from us and even from the people themselves. Appealing to those needs and wants to belong, to be appreciated, or simply to feel safe will bring success.

Chapter 3: Learn Persuasion

Customers do not come to buy a house, a car, or an insurance policy. Rather they are buying security, status, stability, and other intangible things. Salespeople who can pick up these intangibles and address them are the ones making the most sales. If we can show that what we have for sale supplies a need or satisfies a want, it is persuasive; if it stimulates ambition or promises prestige, it is persuasive; if it reassures personal security or other contributions to personal well-being, it is persuasive. Our job is to discover what people really want, and help them discover how to get it. When we make them aware, they will move heaven and earth to get it.

We all probably met people who have bought a certain house, car, or watch not for its features, but for the status it conveyed. While talking of safety, durability, or comfort, they silently fuel their self-esteem with the standing those purchases offer.

There is a saying that "buyers are liars." Why? Because people think they know their real needs and wants in a particular situation. They do not mislead intentionally. Their situation may require, for example, a bigger house on a bigger lot for less money, but their personal needs and wants is to belong to a golf playing crowd. They may end up buying a smaller house on a tiny lot in a Country Club from another realtor because that realtor recognizes and helps them to fulfill their *real* need.

All human behavior, at its root, is driven by the need

to avoid pain and expand pleasure. Therefore, there are, basically, only two things that motivate people—inspiration or desperation. Successful persuaders understand what customers associate with pain and pleasure and use both to make them act and fulfill their unmet needs and wants. Eric Hoffer said, *"The real persuaders are our appetites, our fears, and above all our vanity. The skillful propagandist stirs and coaches these internal persuaders."*

According to Abraham Maslow, a renowned psychologist who first introduced the hierarchy of needs, humans have the following needs: physiological, safety, social, esteem, and self-actualization. Maslow's hierarchy is a model of human needs that allows to discover what is universal and what is unique about each customer and to tap into the needs and fears we all share. Fortunately people have similar personal needs. Uniqueness of each person is reflected in the difference of importance of the same basic needs. Different people buy for different reasons. They ask themselves different questions: How much I need it, how badly I want it, and how much I will be protected? How I will feel, how proud I will be, how others will think of me? Maybe not in those exact words, maybe even not consciously.

We have to understand these questions and find out customers' place on the hierarchy of needs. If we can place customers at a particular level of the pyramid of needs, we can read across and find the basic motivation associated with that need.

Chapter 3: Learn Persuasion

Our job is to **discover** customers' *real* wants and needs, **design** a persuasive message that motivates them to take the desired action, and skillfully **deliver** the message with passion.

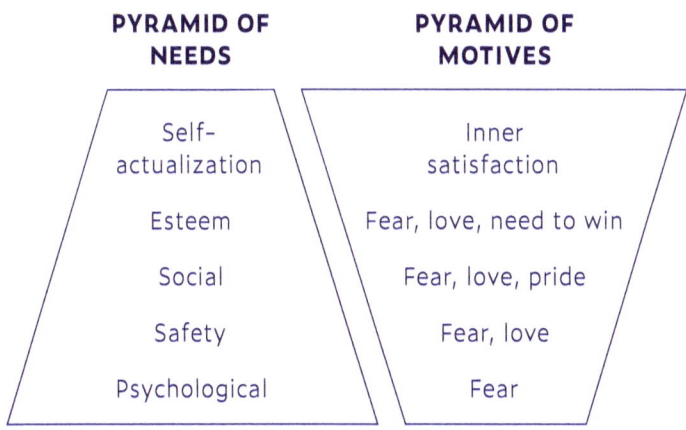

Maslow's ideas provide with means of interpreting, arousing, and influencing the behaviors of customers. Moving up the pyramid one's needs become more complex, and so do the motives.

We should set customers' minds at rest by telling them they are making a right decision. It may be reassurances or guaranties at lower levels, and it may be making them feel as achievers or belonging to a certain group at higher levels. Something like, *"I know you are going to enjoy and feel safe living in this house,"* or, *"Your friends will approve this purchase,"* may be appropriate. To persuade effectively, uncover and address your customers' lowest unmet need in the pyramid, and then show them how to meet that need. People will buy what they *need* from people who understand what they *want*. Whatever the need is, there is always a solution. Persuasion is just to match the two and motivate people to act.

So, do not think what you can sell them, think what you can help them with to satisfy their needs. By thinking in terms of customers needs, you remain flexible in finding ways to meet them. The art of persuasion is all about identifying needs and motives. It is a need to better customers' lives that matters, our products and services are just the means to satisfy the need.

Learn to Find the Right Appeal

People have different personalities, different dominant senses, and different needs. We have to learn how to appeal to each. In any persuasion effort we should suit the style and tone of an appeal to the purpose and the customer.

There are three basic ways to appeal to customers:
- Appeal to logic
- Appeal to emotions
- Appeal to ethics

These are not mutually exclusive, and depending on the problems and people involved the three ways may be used in different combinations. Combining appeals makes our efforts more powerful and, eventually, successful. Which appeal to use, which one should be dominant, and in which combinations to use them depends on the customers we are dealing with and also upon what we are selling. Remember, whenever decision is made, it is mostly emotion that determines the outcome.

Logic

A **logical appeal** is a method of persuasion based on evidence and reasoning. When persuading homeowners to let me list their homes, I present logical reasons for hiring me. Appeal to reason is powerful because it relies on truth. I tell them about my experience, my education, my knowledge of the subject, my company and our advertising and Internet presence, and so on. I provide logical reasoning, facts, and statistics. There are many logical reasons to go ahead, and the chances of success depend a lot on whether my arguments make sense.

Knowing what causes people to make the decisions they make, I understand that a simple good argument may not be enough to win customers over. Customers think that they buy because they have the facts and "know" what they want. It would be great if we could, in the words of Aristotle, "fight our case with no help beyond the bare facts." But given what human nature is, Aristotle implies that emotional and ethical appeals have to be applied alongside logic.

Emotion

An **emotional appeal** is a method of persuasion based on customer's needs, values, and emotional sensibilities.

In selling a house, for example, I might emphasize an emotional appeal of status and demonstration of love for their family. The appeal to emotions plays often the most significant role, depending on what people buy and what are their personalities. When deciding, people want to feel good about their decision. By using highly emotionally charged words, examples, and stories I give them the feeling that, in hiring me, they are making the right choice.

Ethics

An **ethical appeal** is a method of persuasion based on the salesperson's character, credibility, and consistency. Bad reputation will undermine the most logical appeal whereas a good one may compensate for holes in logic. In high priced purchases, like a house, customers want to feel confident that they are dealing with a trustworthy person. No customer wants to deal with a crook whose only concern is commission. Trust is more needed in sales than ever.

If people do not know us, we have to tell them about our expertise, experience, and integrity. Our entire presentation should convey our trustworthiness and why we are the ones to work with. This appeal must present us as a trustworthy source of information. A persuasive ethical appeal helps customers to decide to buy: *"We will analyze the market to find the right price, and will negotiate to obtain the best possible price. Working with professional inspectors and appraisers, we will assure that the house worth the money you are paying."*

To apply a right combination of appeals, we have to understand people and their problems. Every sale consists of people, and every sale has problems. To become successful persuaders, we have to study people and understand human psyche. We have to apply that knowledge to a particular customer. But mostly, the persuasion effort has to focus on problems; they are much easier to mend than people. Persuading means changing how people look at problems and making them see we are the solution to their problems. It doesn't mean changing who they are.

Practice Makes Perfect What We Have Learned

Understanding personality types, NLP, and Maslow's hierarchy of needs, we can acquire new skills that would allow us to appeal successfully to different people. By learning new skills, finding the opportunities to practice them, and consciously using these skills every day could help us develop them. When you have learned a particular skill, apply it in real life situations. *Applied* knowledge is power. Knowledge is what we acquire; what we do with it is wisdom. Obtain necessary knowledge and practice, practice, and practice. Learning without practicing is like planting seeds and then just show up to harvest the yield. We have to practice each day persuasion techniques, and apply them until they become as natural as breathing. We have to have fundamentals so firmly in our minds they become part of us.

There are many opportunities to practice the learned skills at home, at work, and in the community. To master these skills, there is no better exercise than to decide what we want to achieve and consciously go after it. Look for examples of persuasion in your daily experiences and chances to practice.

> "What we learn to do, we learn by doing."
> — ARISTOTLE

For example:

- Persuade a child to complete homework
- Persuade a family member to take a new household responsibility
- Persuade a spouse to see a movie you want
- Persuade a client to extend a deadline
- Persuade a colleague to substitute for you
- Persuade neighbors to join you for a cause
- Persuade your home owner association to allow something you want

Persuasion skills, like all skills, are developed through practice, feedback, and extra practice. As in any fitness program, progress will depend on *regular* and *consistent* practice. *Extra* practice is the difference between ordinary and extraordinary. Having skills is one thing; using them is another.

Chapter 3: Learn Persuasion

Immediately after applying a new skill while it is fresh in the mind, think about what worked and what did not work and what should have or should not have been said. Then decide how to improve and take what you have learned to the next opportunity.

Every person has the potential to master persuasion. Do not be daunted by the whole picture, just take one step at a time. It is wisely said that the journey of a thousand miles begins with simple step. Although at first we may fail, if we persevere in the practice, we will become progressively better. With learning and practicing persuasion skills, we can gradually break through inability to lead people. Like water seeping through the crack in a dam, eventually, the "mental" dam will give up and subconscious competence will freely flow.

Reading about persuasion alone will not boost your ability to convince. Do not just read; learn, practice, and, above all, act.

CHAPTER 4

Rapport and Persuasion

"Rapport equals trust plus comfort."

— NEIL STRAUSS

What Is Rapport and Why Is It Important?

Dictionary defines rapport as a state of harmony between two people. My favorite description of it is "respect for each other's model of the world."

Rapport is a process of building a relationship based on mutual understanding, respect, and trust. In the process, customers "get" us; more important, the feeling is mutual—they feel we "get" them. We are to be with them on the same wavelength mentally and emotionally, joining them where they are rather than forcing them to go where we want. It makes everyone feel they are on the same side of the fence and on the same page. That not only helps us to sell but also makes it easier for customers to buy. That is why building rapport with a prospect has to be our first objective.

Of course, customers will not be easily convinced and take at face value anything salespeople say just because of rapport, but they may have a tendency to believe, and that may help us to convince them.

Rapport helps us:

- To put customer at ease
- To lower resistance
- To be liked
- To lead

Customers will not deal with us as salespeople unless they get a good feel for us as people. That is why rapport is necessary in sales.

Rapport Is Not a Nicety, It Is a Necessity

Even the finest seeds will not take root or bear fullest fruit if the soil is uncultivated. Cultivate rapport; it is your pass to greater profits. It is like money; with it we can get what we want, without connection we go broke. So, take care of the interaction from the very minute the meeting with a prospect starts. From the introduction to the closing, through information we communicate verbally and non-verbally, we must establish a bond that leads to the desired outcome. Although the buying decision is revealed at the end of the selling process, it is being cultivated throughout.

Do not leave rapport up to fate like amateur salespeople do. Professional salespeople know that it is not a mere social nicety but a perfect setting for their persuasion efforts that facilitate more responsive reaction to suggestions.

Rapport is not a detour but a necessity when trying to bond with people.

Like lubricating oil reduces friction, connection makes every subsequent step in the persuasion process smoother, easier, and more likely to succeed. Lack of rapport usually causes excessive resistance and, because of it, disappointment.

Make a Conscious Effort to Establish Rapport

While interacting, we can influence each other's behavior, including breathing, heart rate, and blood pressure. It may happen naturally and subconsciously. For some people, rapport comes naturally; they are subconsciously competent, connecting with people without thinking what they are doing. The majority of us can still build some rapport naturally and subconsciously. Think of different facial expressions and tone of voice we use subconsciously when we congratulate someone or express condolences. However, by bringing rapport into conscious, we can become more adept at it.

Establishing rapport, if it doesn't come naturally to you, is most effective when done consciously by employing different techniques and being flexible enough to accommodate different people. Bringing rapport techniques into consciousness, with practice, we can become subconsciously competent as well.

Selling Is Persuading

First, we would have to move from being subconsciously incompetent—not recognizing that we cannot establish rapport—to being consciously incompetent—recognizing we have difficulties establishing rapport naturally and have to work on it. Understanding there is much we do not know is the beginning of real growth by developing necessary means. By practicing these techniques, we become consciously competent—being aware of what we are doing and effective at it. With further practice, acquired techniques will become so natural they sink into subconscious, and we will become consciously unaware of what we are doing. We will reach the level of subconscious competence. In short, we move from the unknown unknowns to the known unknowns to the known knowns to doing it without consciously thinking about it.

There are many ways to consciously working on establishing rapport. Initially we may feel overwhelmed by having to think about bonding. However, like any skill, with practice we will do what is necessary without thinking. It's like driving. At first we have to think about our every action: turn this, press that, shift something else. Consciously building rapport by mastering necessary means and then letting them fade into subconscious, it becomes natural and intuitive, but built on a foundation of scientifically developed skills.

Chapter 4: Rapport and Persuasion

Means to Establish Rapport

- **Genuinely and sincerely care about customers.**

    Rapport is more easily established when we sincerely try to understand the customers, how they think and what they feel. The attention we pay to the customers' concerns creates rapport because we show understanding, empathy, and acceptance.

- **Be at the same level as customers.**

    As a teacher, I learned to sit at the same level as a student when I wanted cooperation. When I needed to project power I had a student sit while I stood. Talking down to customers, literally and figuratively, does not work in sales; what works is being at the same level. When dressing, showing off your expertise, and constructing sentences, be just a notch above your customers to project authority.

- **Be in sync with customers.**

    Synchronicity creates rapport. When two people are in rapport, they move as one, as if they are dancing. Psychologists have found that the more two people naturally make coordinated moves when conversing, the greater their positive feelings; just like in a dance. As to tango,

Selling Is Persuading

we need two people moving in sync, so facial expressions, flashing eyebrows, rapid gestures, and words pacing during a conversation have to be synchronized. Once we are in sync with dance partners or customers, we can lead the interaction.

- **Be likeable**

   Unlike animals, people, in most cases, especially when they want someone to part with hard-earned money, do not gain success by being aggressive but by being kind and therefore likeable. Being likeable means you are pleasant and comfortable to be around. Being liked requires effort. As tough as it to achieve physical fitness, it is tough to achieve likeability that is a kind of social fitness. One of the best ways to get customers like us is to get them feel we are just about like them. People want to feel good about themselves, and are subconsciously attracted to traits and words close to their own. Familiarity and likability breed business.

Become a salesperson that customers enjoy doing business with.

People like and gravitate to those who are similar to them. The similarity principle is as compelling in psychology as gravity is in physics. To paraphrase Newton's law of

Chapter 4: Rapport and Persuasion

gravity, we may say that people are attracted to each other with a force directly proportional to their similarities and inversely proportional to the square of their differences. In the lay language it means that the more similar we are to our customers, the more comfortable they are with us; the more foreign we seem, the less we succeed.

Attraction is present everywhere in the universe—gravity, magnetism, electrical charges; matter is held together by attraction. Attraction in human interaction also holds everything together and is, largely, caused by similarity. The notion that opposites attract is a myth, and can be applied to charged particles and magnets, not, usually, to humans. Similarity between humans engenders harmony; difference tends to result in turmoil.

Rapport to sales is like harmony to music. No harmony—no music, no rapport—no sale and no referrals Being in harmony does not mean that everyone plays the same melody. In an orchestra, the different instruments mix while each plays its own part. Just as different but harmonious notes played together force the music forward so some differences in people's thoughts and ideas compel reevaluation and move the interaction forward. It means we need not agree at *everything* to feel connected. Rapport and agreement are not the same.

During the interaction, customers receive a great deal of information about salespeople through different sensory channels, and they form powerful impressions. People are constantly evaluating multiple pieces of information at once and deciding about them outside of the conscious. Nothing escapes them as they absorb the information they need to decide whether to do business with us. Never underestimate customers' instinctive ability to read your body language. Let your posture, gait, and facial impression show confidence, even if it is not how you feel. Being confident, caring, and considerate, we will be perceived as more capable, intelligent, and attractive. That will put customers at ease.

When with customers, salespeople, much like actors, are always on stage. As actors, they have to look, sound, and act the part of an expert and present themselves in ways that make the desired impression. As actors, they also have to open sensory channels to see, hear, and feel how the audience (customers) reacts. Their reactions with facial expressions, gestures, and body postures let us know if the "act" is working.

Rapport Starts with a Proper Introduction

In reality, introduction starts before the introduction proper because information is conveyed not only verbally and consciously but also nonverbally and subconsciously.

Subconsciously, people are more persuaded by attractive people. They make instant judgments about us based on many criteria, and, although it is unfair, attractiveness is one of them. But attractiveness is not just being beautiful or handsome. It is also an overall appearance, by which

Chapter 4: Rapport and Persuasion

people immediately form impressions. Appearance is always sending out a message and declaring a position, persuades and connotes, suggests and insinuates. It is judged by clothing, footwear, and hairstyle. Even if we go naked, it says something to the world. What is true about closing is also true about accessories, briefcases, watches, automobiles, etc. When people meet you for the first time, they will treat you in accordance with how you package yourself: your attire and grooming, your gait, and your handshake.

When we are well dressed and groomed, customers subconsciously assume that we are professionals, and take us, and the persuasion to follow, more seriously.

Look persuasively, appearance affects perception of authority and professionalism.

One overlooked benefit of looking good is how it makes us feel. Dressing professionally makes us feel like professionals, and walking confidently makes us more confident. Confidence and professionalism affects persuasiveness.

Often, when buying a book, people are persuaded not by the table of content but by the book's jacket that really is a "fable of content." We all know those people who say it is wrong to judge a book by its jacket and people by their dress. Forget them. Right or wrong, people are more easily persuaded by those who dress well. Customers are flattered when we dress up for the meeting; they feel, most of the time subconsciously, that we consider them important enough to dress up. If we give people the feeling of importance that everyone, at least subconsciously, craves for, they will listen to us favorably. Just do not overdress; wearing a tuxedo or shorts, to show a house looks silly. The idea is not to differ too much from customers, but to increase our status slightly so we command attention and project authority by dressing a notch above them.

After impressing with your appearance, treat the introduction as a mini presentation. Do not let the stress of meeting a new customer lead to rushing through the introduction. Complement the impression with a friendly handshake. A handshake is the first and often the only physical contact salespeople have with customers. Most sales encounters allow two handshakes—at the beginning and after the meeting—so make both count. If appropriate, a casual touch in between involves the sense of touch. The more senses you involve, the better. Each engaged sense helps to break the barrier that separates you from the prospect.

But whether we are introducing ourselves or closing the sale, touching customers (in a subtle and appropriate way) subconsciously activates the human desire to bond by imparting sense of caring and connection. In sales situations it is often best to "touch" a customer with a genuine smile or verbally by offering a compliment.

When shaking hands:

- **Let the customer be the first to offer a hand**

Chapter 4: Rapport and Persuasion

The person with higher status initiates the shake. We want to make our customers feel important.

- **Make sure your hands are not sweating**

    Do not wipe them in front of a person you are about to shake hands with.

- **Make eye contact**

    It is the most important part of a handshake. Not making eye contact when we ought to can have devastating results. Ralph Waldo Emerson said, *"The eyes of men converse as much as their tongues."*

- **Slightly lean forward and smile**

    If a handshake says *"Nice to see you,"* a smile says *"I like you."* A smile is an immediately built bridge to another person and ambassador of peace and good will. It not only shows we are pleased meeting customers, but also reassures and conveys confidence, enthusiasm, and acceptance. A pleasant expression and a genuine smile put the best face forward, and face is the place that most people focus on first to evaluate us. *"Smile,"* said Andre Maurois *"for everyone lacks self-confidence and more than any other thing a smile reassures them."* Customers trust more salespeople who express their emotions through a dynamic and enthusiastic face. Remember that the genuine smile does not start at the lips, but rather in the eyes.

- **Always offer your hand vertically**

    Hand offered palm down is domineering, and palm up is submissive.

- **Use a firm handshake**

    Do not grasp just the fingers. Engage the palm, but not with a crushing grip. A firm handshake suggests cooperation; weak one conveys just that—weakness.

- **Attach your name to the greeting**

    "Hello, I am Jacob." Repeat the customer's name a few times, *"Sabina. Glad to meet you, Sabina."* Not only you will remember the names better, but because the sound of their names is the sweetest to customers' ears, you build up rapport. Remembering and using customers' name is one of the fastest ways to form an immediate bond with them. Never forget your customer's name, and, by the way, never let the customer forget yours. Make yourself memorable. Find ways to be surprising and unique. Prospects are begging for someone to stand out and solve their problems.

Chapter 4: Rapport and Persuasion

Often, on a second meeting, people call me Joseph instead of Jacob. I used it to my advantage. Now, when introducing myself, I tell, "I am Jacob, although people are sometimes calling me Joseph. I think it is because they are both biblical names and both start with a J. I hate to correct people." Customers not only remember my name, they also remember *me* as a guy who hates to correct them.

By the amount of eye contact during the handshake, firmness, duration, and type of grip, we could communicate strength or weakness, concern or indifference, warmth or aloofness.

Establishing rapport starts with an introduction, but it's only the beginning of the process.

Small Talk: The Appetizer

As the main course is usually preceded by an appetizer, business communication is typically preceded by small talk. Small talk is really a search for basis of connection. It helps people get accustomed to each other's mood, speaking style, and energy level.

Exchanges at the beginning of meetings facilitate transitions into "big talk." Icebreakers cover the slightly awkward moments of settling down and settling in, and shape interaction by building rapport. To build rapport, learn how to connect with anyone, anywhere, anytime.

After introduction:

- **Express appreciation**

    "Thank you for taking the time to see me today, Mr. Customer."

- **Offer a drink when you have an opportunity**

    Hot coffee is better than cold water. Subconsciously, people will judge us as warmer and more sincere.

- **Keep the conversation light**

    Do not talk business in the first few minutes. If you rush into business discussion without establishing rapport, you may have an unpleasant experience, or even worse, an unsatisfactory outcome. Talk about the weather, the traffic, or some other light subject. Connect first as a person rather than as a salesperson.

- **Find common ground with customers**

    Commonality makes a difference. Uncover something you share—hobbies, acquaintances, or interests. Rapport is created by discovering and, when needed, creating commonality. Similarity leads to liking. Look for at least one point of commonality and use it often; it is all that is needed to create a bond. After discovering that

Chapter 4: Rapport and Persuasion

we have similarities unrelated to the business at hand, there are more to talk about.

"I see you belong to Toastmasters International, too. Which club? That's a good club. Have you ever heard about my club at... ?"

We can talk in the same manner about sports, same schools we attended, or states we lived in.

"Do you like baseball? Hey, so do I! Who do you think will win this week?"

- **Offer a compliment**

    When we compliment people and make them feel good about themselves and important, we can persuade them to do many things. *"I can live for two months on a good compliment,"* Mark Twain said. When I attend a listing appointment at a nicely decorated house I usually tell *"I have to say, I really like how you decorated your house."* If they did it themselves, they are pleased with the compliment. If not, they are flattered I thought so. A compliment is to be succinct, specific, and sincere.

- **Do not force the small talk**

    If it is not sincere, it does not bring people closer; some people do not like unsolicited small talk.

Selling Is Persuading

During small talk be on the lookout for clues that will indicate what customers are comfortable with: formal versus informal, open versus closed, high energy versus low energy, positive perspective versus negative perspective, etc. We can learn a lot by observing customers while talking with them: their personality type, sensory preferences, and desires. This knowledge allows finding the right approach. That is why small talk and observational skills are important.

Always be sensitive to how small talk is being received and when it's time to move on. Once we have gotten good at starting small talk, we have to practice the transition to business conversation (big talk). Some people are good at breaking the ice, but when it comes to the "big talk" they become too serious, and the change in behavior confuses, if only subconsciously, customers.

When we find ourselves where small talk is not working, there are other ways to establish rapport by reducing differences between us and customers with "artificial" means. The most important are mirroring and matching.

Mirroring and Matching

Behaving like the people we are talking to and consciously taking on someone's style are powerful techniques of creating rapport. It is a powerful concept that people like people similar to them; and similarity can be created by mirroring or matching. Synchronizing by mirroring and matching customers in language, voice, breathing rate,

Chapter 4: Rapport and Persuasion

emotional state, energy level, and mood, we speed up connecting, get into rapport, and convert likeness into liking. As for a mirror to reflect the reality correctly, it has to be clear, smooth, and flat, so our sensory channels has to be open to correctly observe customers so we see, hear, feel, and understand their verbal and nonverbal messages.

There is a subtle difference between the two. It is in the degree of emulation. Mirroring means we become a mirroring image of a person. If the person tilts the head to the left, we tilt the head to the right, like the person would see in a mirror. While mirroring is a precise reflection, matching is a more general image of the other person. When mirroring words of another person, we use the same words; when matching, we use similar words.

Everyone has the ability to mirror and match to some degree; it is a natural human resource. People often involuntarily mirror others. We sit down, for example, to talk to people sitting and stand when they are standing. The drive to emulate is hardwired into the brain. Emulating leads to cooperation and survival. It is also an ancient method of learning we find even in the animal world. Youngsters, both human and animal, imitate adults. Our task is methodically developing this natural ability. To succeed in sales, we need to *deliberately* improve our mirroring and matching techniques. Once we have begun to consciously and, *consequently*, subconsciously blend our style with our customers' style, we will sell more.

Selling Is Persuading

The subject of conscious mirroring and matching is thoroughly explored by Neuro-Linguistic Programming (NLP). NLP is only making explicit what we do naturally, and uncovers techniques that successful communicators use to build and maintain rapport with customers by:

- Reflecting speaking patterns, tone, and the loudness of their voices.
- Adopting their style and rhythm in speech, movement, and breathing.
- Using similar postures, gestures, and facial expressions.
- Making use of the same phrases. Listen for people using visual, auditory, or kinesthetic words. *"That looks great," "That sounds promising,"* and *"That feels good"* are the clues that customers may be most receptive to information in visual, verbal, or tactile way.

A while ago, I was sitting in the club house of a development where I was farming (cultivating prospects). The president of the men's club walked in. We had seen each other a few times, but nothing outside of greeting was exchanged.

I wanted to befriend him. I stood up with a friendly smile and open arms.

"Hello there," he said.

Matching his body posture and tone of voice, I echoed,

Chapter 4: Rapport and Persuasion

"Hello there."

*"I have **seen** you in the development a couple of times," he added, "And I have received your postcards. You **look** exactly as on the cards."*

*From his use of visual words and quick talk, I concluded that he was a Visual. "You **see**, I don't want to surprise people when I meet them, so I keep my **picture** current," I answered also using visual words and mirroring his gestures and facial expression. We spoke for a couple of minutes in this manner when he finally said, "You know something? Why don't you give me a call so we can talk about you coming to one of our meetings and speak about real estate?"*

It amused me how well NLP worked.

More often than not, the difference between success and failure in sales is in the way people communicate. Every time we communicate with words, we are also sending messages nonverbally whether we are aware of them or not. Rapport between people is created as much by the spoken language as by body language. When we observe and listen carefully to people and communicate with them in the same verbal and nonverbal language, they will hear us, feel comfortable with us, and be more open to us.

To become proficient at emulating we need to develop keen observation and flexibility and practice; practice observing and understanding what others feel, think, and say. It is a skill, and, as with any other skill, it takes practice to develop. If conscious mirroring is new to you, begin in situations where there is practically no risk. Try it with a bank teller or a cashier, and start by mirroring one thing like gestures or voice. After some practice it becomes less conscious and eventually subconscious.

Mirroring and Matching Versus Mimicking

While reflecting people's behavior, be careful not to imitate. They could feel manipulated. There is a fine distinction between imitation and emulation, and the difference between mimicking and mirroring/matching is often a matter of degree. We walk a fine line when establishing rapport because mirroring and matching works well if it is covert. Salvador Dali said, *"The secret of my influence has always been that it remained secret."*

When we approximate people's body language, they subconsciously sense we are in harmony with them. But when they catch us mimicking, they sense manipulation. Instead of directly mimicking, we can just match the overall tone and manner of customers.

When people:

- Cross their legs, we can cross our arms
- Tap their fingers, we may tap a pen
- Lean their head one way, we can do it the other way

- Repeatedly nod their heads, we can move our hands in a similar rhythm

However, do not match customers' counterproductive behavior. When customers become angry, nothing is gained by responding in a similar manner.

When we are in rapport with customers—breathing with them, moving with them, thinking the way they do—we are not mimicking them, we are making them feel understood at a very basic level. Rapport is about behavioral flexibility, not compromising our identity.

Tune Your Dial to the Customer's Wavelength

In physics there is a phenomenon called resonance. It is best illustrated by two pendulums of the same length, mounted side by side that would swing together in precise rhythm even if they start not being in sync. The same phenomenon is used when we turn the dial to tune up to a particular radio station and synchronize the wavelength of the radio receiver with the wavelength emitted by the intended radio station. When waves synchronize, they amplify. When they are out of sync, they cancel each other.

People also have the capacity for resonance—an emotional resonance—and they also tend to move in precise, shared synchronicity with each other. When we synchronize the verbal and nonverbal components of our communication with those of our customers, we amplify rapport; when we botch synchronicity, we cancel out rapport. If resonance is to be achieved, we need to alter our approach to be on the same wavelength as our customers. The wiring for such resonance seems built into the human brain.

All these techniques are important, but if we match our customers speaking patterns, mirror their movements, and synchronizing our breathing, nothing much would happen. When we have established rapport using different techniques, it is time to start to slowly lead them to see and accept our viewpoint. The whole idea of establishing rapport is to be able to lead customers.

Last but not least, rapport works best not as a selling technique, but as a lifestyle, a philosophy—a way of connecting with people.

CHAPTER 5

Rules of Persuasion

"Persuasion is often more effectual than force."

— AESOP

Persuasion Is Not Only an Art, It Is a Science

Just as science is regulated by laws, persuasion is regulated by rules. There are no laws of persuasion, only rules we, usually either consciously or subconsciously, obey. The main difference between laws of nature and rules of persuasion is these laws are unbreakable and universal, but rules can be broken, though at our own peril.

When people talk and write about changing minds, they often quote Newton's third law of motion: *For every action there is an equal and opposite reaction.* Being trained in physical science, I have explored the possibility of modification and application of all three of Newton's laws to persuasion and concluded that all can be modified and applied to the psychological world. I tested this theory in the real world and came up with three rules of persuasion analogous to the laws of motion.

Three is not an arbitrary number. Aristotle, who wrote one of the first great treatises on persuasion, argued that successful persuasion requires three elements: **ethos** (trust), **logos** (logic), **and pathos** (emotion). These ideas are as fresh now as the day they were written. While persuasion is an ancient art, now it is much more subtle and complex. In modern terms, applied to sales, that means that success requires establishing trust through personal packaging, presenting the case with indisputable logic, and giving a tug to customers' emotions.

Any of the three elements are important. But it is essential to remember that in this triad customers are the most important part. They must change attitudes, decide, and take actions because of our persuasion effort.

The rules of persuasion are based on the following three elements:

1. **Characteristics of the persuader**

    Persuasion usually is credibility driven, and trust is one of the most valuable thing salespeople can share with customers. It allows customers to rely on their expertise and save time and energy otherwise spent to figure out everything by themselves.

2. **Psychological context within which the persuasion takes place**

    Persuasion does not occur in a vacuum. In any particular situation many factors can affect the outcome. Our arguments must make perfect sense for a particular customer in a particular situation.

3. **Mind-set of the persuadee**

    Arguments must appeal to the customers' emotional side. Fair and effective use of emotional appeal is often the difference between successful and failed presentation.

The three rules of persuasion are based respectively on these three elements.

The First Rule of Persuasion

The first Newton's law of motion, often called the law of inertia, says that *to change the state of a physical body a force must be applied*. The body in motion stays in motion, and the body at rest stays at rest.

Inertia is both physical and psychological phenomenon. It is hard to get things going, both physically and psychologically, and it is difficult to speed them up, slow them down, and change directions. The first rule of persuasion, therefore, is *to change a state of human mind a psychological force must be applied.* If we can "force" a customer to gradually move in the right direction, we will generate positive momentum.

A force can be deadly if applied improperly. Persuasion will fail if we try to bend customers to our will. When we and our customers get locked into a war of the wills, we always lose. Lose because ideas are not accepted when forced from the outside. *"The fool tells me his reasons,"* Aristotle said, *"The wise man persuades me with my own."*

Suggestions are absorbed only if they come from within. We have to gently "force" customers toward what we know and they suspect will benefit them. This gentle "force" should help to persuade customers, but it should never be presented as a force somehow superior to their wants and needs. Persuasion involves influence, but never actual force, and is more powerful than official power.

It is difficult to say how far we should go and to what extent we have an obligation to persuade customers to buy what we think will better their lives. Some things are obvious, others are not. But unless we make them want to go where we want them to go, they will resist. Our job is to make them realize that what we offer is in their interest. The trick is to get customers see the ideas we want them to accept as their own. Persuasion is the ability to affect customers *as if* without exertion of external force using scientifically proven techniques.

The only persuasive force that salespeople can exert to accomplish a sale without destroying the relationship is the force of credibility determined by *perceived* expertise and trustworthiness.

Sources of such force are:
- **Information**—provide provable facts
- **Knowledge**—demonstrate expertise
- **Skills**—promote techniques
- **Reputation**—use testimonials and references
- **Confidence**—show poise. To be persuasive, you must be confident.

Although the linkage between persuasion and these characteristics is complex, the conclusion is simple; to lead people we must be trustworthy experts.

To have customers to say "yes" two conditions must be met.

The **first condition** is to make customers see us as competent enough to meet their needs. We have to be—and, what is even more important, have customers see us as—experts in our fields.

Expertise, besides interpersonal and listening skills we discussed earlier, includes product knowledge. Product knowledge, besides knowing everything about your product, also includes knowledge of your competitors' products. Understanding the benefits, drawbacks, and price comparison of all products in your field helps answer customers' questions and aids in pairing a customer with a right product.

Selling Is Persuading

Customers trust experts; most important, they buy from them. So, do not be shy to let people know you are good at what you do. If you want to be recognized as an expert, promote yourself. The easiest way to let customers know that you are an expert is to tell them. You can tell people about your accomplishments by using stories, testimonials, or statistics.

The following anecdote illustrates the importance of expertise.

> *Once, a priest offered a nun a ride home. Entering the car, she pulled up her robe so her knees were exposed. The priest barely avoided a crash. Taking control of the car, he puts his hand on her knee. The nun says: "Father, do you remember psalm 129?"*
>
> *The priest takes his hand away, but in a while does it again. The nun repeats: "Father, do you remember psalm 129?"*
>
> *The priest apologizes: "Sorry sister, but flesh is weak."*
>
> *At the monastery, the disappointed nun leaves the car.*
>
> *Returning to the church, the priest finds psalm 129. It says, Go higher and seek. Higher you will find happiness.*

The moral is, if we don't know our trade well, opportunities will be missed.

If we are not seen as experts, there are two ways to deal with low perceived competence:

Chapter 5: Rules of Persuasion

- Become more competent.
- Change perception of our competence. In sales, seeming is more important than being.

There is only one way to become more competent—study and practice.

And few things could be done to change customers' perceptions. It is the people's *perception* of our expertise that matters. Perceptions control how people respond to something, and we have control over their perceptions. We may be competent, but if we do not seem confident, we lose the battle.

Let's see what can be done to influence the perception.

1. Moving fast and with confidence, as we have places to go and people to see, we project professionalism. When we move, we have to move with precision, assuring customers we know what we are doing. Acting as if we are more confident than we feel, we not only portraying ourselves as being self-assured, we are feeling and becoming more confident. Forcing ourselves to act a certain way, we become the way we act. We are the act, so we must act with care.

2. Maintaining eye contacts and speaking with confidence, we send signals we are sure of

Selling Is Persuading

ourselves. Authoritatively talking, although not always knowing more than the people who talk hesitantly, we create an impression of confidence and are *perceived* to be more competent and credible. People bow to confidence and naturally associate it with expertise. What is behind the self-confidence is secondary to the *perception* it creates. Confidence increases the ability to persuade. Be confident, but do not be arrogant.

3. The posture and body language should communicate confidence. Fake it until you make it. In sales—some might say in life—there is always acting. As a salesperson, sometimes imagine that you are an actor playing a role and act. How we see ourselves as salespeople, so do our customers; and when we change how we see ourselves, the salespeople our customers see will change also.

4. Including statistics is a highly effective way of ensuring that what we say is credible, even if they are mostly meaningless. It creates the illusion of expertise also. Use precise figures; people believe precise figures more than they believe rounded numbers.

5. Professional jargon could be similarly persuasive. Although everyone claims to hate jargon,

Chapter 5: Rules of Persuasion

the truth is if we are to give the impression of being an expert, jargon often helps. People are persuaded by someone they perceive to have a specialized knowledge they do not. Just do not overdo it. Know when to use, and not use, professional jargon. While you may know what you are talking about, you cannot count that your customers understand you when you overdo it.

With these techniques we would project a sense of certainty. Research indicates that people buy from those who seem certain about what they are doing and what they are saying. There is no quality as compelling, intoxicating, and attractive as certainty. If we send off signals of self-assurance about what we do, we can always persuade others to do what is right for them, while getting what we need. Customers will perceive us as competent and consistent if we act with confidence but not conceit, comfort but not contempt, certainty but not condescendingly.

The **second condition** for successful persuasion is to make customers trust us. We cannot share our expertise if customers do not trust us and are not willing to talk to us. Expertise does not equal trust. Trust is one quality that leads to compliance provided it has been established before the request is made.

Whenever we try to lead, customers, consciously or subconsciously, ask themselves: Can I trust this person?

Selling Is Persuading

Do I believe this person? Is the person concerned about me? In this new world, never assume that customers trust us. If in the past people trusted others until they gave them a reason not to, now, they do not trust until we prove that we are trustworthy. To succeed at persuasion, we must earn and build up trust, and do it quickly. Trustworthy people perceived as capable, consistent, and caring. People must believe in us before they believe us; our approach should be first as a people, then as salespeople. When salespeople lack integrity, their words are discounted no matter how knowledgeable, smart, and eloquent they are. But remember that customers do not appreciate ethical salespeople without having the requisite competence.

Trustworthiness is based on such qualities as perceived:

- Intelligence
- Honesty
- Dependability
- Maturity
- Enthusiasm
- Good judgment

All the knowledge in the world will not generate sales and will not convert prospects into customers and customers into clients if they do not trust us. Trust opens up people and makes them explore what we can do for them; lack of trust and belief we can do nothing for them makes people close their minds.

Chapter 5: Rules of Persuasion

Sales and clients are made when trust exists.

Usually, people trust those with an established reputation or who they have relationships with. That is why it pays off to establish a reputation with consistent marketing and to establish relationships with future clients.

As trust in us and confidence in our expertise rises, fear disappears, and customers say "yes." If they say "no," it means that one or both conditions have not been met.

Besides trust and expertise, likeability also helps. This triad—perceived expertise, trust, and likeability—not only makes for customers easy to agree with us, but do so without careful consideration.

Ask yourself:

- Do your customers believe you know what you are talking about?
- Do they believe that you are trustworthy?

Don't be afraid to demonstrate or market your qualifications—they confer expertise; don't be afraid to use testimonials and third party endorsements—they confer trustworthiness.

Additional questions should be asked:

- Do your customers like you and feel comfortable with you?
- Besides being credible are you appealing?

Selling Is Persuading

If the answer to the questions is *yes,* then you will succeed as a persuader.

Also, a great force in persuasion is self-interest. Self is an important part of self-interest. *"If you would persuade,"* said Benjamin Franklin, *"you must appeal to interest rather intellect."* It is based on a psychological premise that self-interest is a dominant motive in people's behavior. Sad but true, customers are only interested in how our offers apply to them. If that is so, then we have to structure our argument so it is in customers' best interest and position our offer so it is compelling to them. Show what they will gain from what you offer, but focus more on what they will save (headache, heartache, money, time, energy, etc.).

Once we hit the button of self-interest, customers persuade themselves to satisfy their wants and needs; the desire to buy come from within. Nothing is more powerful than customers persuading themselves on salespeople's behalf.

And last, but not least. For salespeople, it is legitimate to care about their self-interest if they are, at least, not working against the interest of customers. We are persuading, convincing, and influencing customers to part with the money they have got for what we have got. It has to be a fair exchange. If we take care of our customers, they will take care of us.

Chapter 5: Rules of Persuasion

The Second Rule of Persuasion

Newton's second law of motion states that Force equals Mass times Acceleration (**F = M x A**). *Force is directly proportional to mass and acceleration.*

Analogous to the second law equation is the persuasion equation: Persuasion equals Observation times Flexibility. (**P = O x F**).

> *Persuasion is directly proportional to how much we observe and how flexible we are to changing our approaches according to the observed facts.*

If you are not into formulas, it just means that the key to influencing people's decisions lies in discovering their motivations by observing them and being flexible to change approaches to reach outcome that satisfies customers and your needs. Selling today requires focus on outcome, judgment, and flexibility.

According to the second rule of persuasion, we can conclude that to become an effective persuader, one must acquire the following three qualities:

1. **Ability to set explicit and verifiable outcomes for every persuasive effort**

    The first element of the equation—persuasion—just as force in Newton's law, has a direction and an explicit outcome. The following story shows

Selling Is Persuading

what could happen when there is no explicit outcome.

A missionary came upon a hungry lion. The missionary knelt and prayed, "God, please give this lion a Christian soul."

The lion stopped, knelt, and prayed also, "Lord above, may this meal be blessed."

Explicit outcome should have been, "God, please save me."

2. **Observational skills to provide feedback about progress toward the outcome**

   The second element—observation—allows us to amass facts about customers. As force is in direct proportion to the mass, so persuasion is in direct proportion to the amount of facts we observed. The more information we input in our heads about our customers, the greater the resources we have to draw upon when persuading them.

3. **Flexibility to change and adjust efforts to achieve the desired outcome**

   The third element—flexibility—is to the change of approaches what acceleration is to the change of speed.

Chapter 5: Rules of Persuasion

Everything about the persuasion force is discussed in previous and subsequent parts of this chapter. So, let's explore the remaining two elements of the equation in depth.

Observation is critical to uncover customer's psychological makeup. After observing a person for a while, we can make a quick psychological sketch in the same way as skilled artists do.

Before we persuade, we need to observe and categorize customers accurately. Otherwise, even the best persuasive tools can backfire. If we hope to be effective at winning customers over, it is vital to discover as much as possible about their traits, preferred mental representations, and needs. Keep your eyes, ears, and minds open at all times. Then we can transform the sketch into a complete psychological portrait and know how to put our case forward: how to present, what words to use, and what buttons to push.

If we have observed that a customer, for example, is a Visual, a Thinker, and concerned with safety, we may say: "As you can **see, statistics show** very **low crime rate** in the area."

Observing means just that, looking and listening without evaluating and picking up the clues. Assuming what is happening in our customers' heads can lead us astray and cause us to judge situations inaccurately. Although it is difficult to observe without judgment when we combine observation with evaluation, people will only hear criticism.

Selling Is Persuading

When observing, use words that describe, not the ones that evaluate. As the name implies, a descriptive word is to provide facts like color, shape, or size; whereas an evaluative word expresses opinion and passes a judgment. With a descriptive word a house can be *expensive*; with evaluative word it becomes *overpriced*. Also, a house can be *vacant* (descriptive) or *abandoned* (evaluative); a customer can be *energetic* (descriptive) or *overbearing* (evaluative).

We often add to what we observed our interpretations based on our experiences. As a result, we have a distorted image, are misinformed, and reach **wrong conclusions**.

The following story that Abraham Lincoln used as a young lawyer is a good reminder not to rush to conclusions.

> *A farmer was sitting on the front porch of his home, when suddenly his 6-year-old son came running from the barn and said, "Father, father, the hired man is in the hayloft with big sister. He is pulling down his pants and she is lifting up her skirt, and I fear they are going to pee on our hay."*
>
> *"Well, son," the farmer said calmly. "You have all the facts right, but your **conclusion** is wrong."*

Do not jump to conclusions. Premature evaluation will not make you last long in sales.

To avoid unnecessary mistakes, we must sharpen our observational skills. Then we will notice *subtle gestures, minute facial expressions, and descriptive words* that will give us a wealth of information beneficial to choosing the right approach. We will notice more subtle but still detectable *changes in skin color, lip tightening, and breathing patterns* and associate them with the corresponding internal states. These fleeting changes may last just a fraction of a second, but once we master the skill of observation, we will be amazed what we can learn about customers' thoughts and feelings and what we can accomplish with this information.

Once we have trained ourselves to seeing and hearing things we would otherwise fail to notice, we will be in a position to "see" the world from our customers' vantage point.

Observation can be done passively, based just on awareness and attention. As Yogi Berra said, *"You can observe just by watching."* Or it can be done actively, based on probing and provoking to elicit a reaction that can reveal a lot of information. We have to ask questions and make customers talk, allowing them to talk without interruption. Then watch, listen, and read the customers in a particular situation, discovering all relevant underlying clues.

If you observe a clue that indicates a particular approach will not achieve success, change that approach. That brings us to the third component of the equation—flexibility.

Flexibility is a way of approaching situations that allows adapting behavior to achieve the desired outcome. Persuading others require an audience, whether it is a single person or group. It is critical to know how to adapt quickly to the audience's needs, wants, and fears. Effective persuasion requires adaptation.

To be flexible:

- Approach customers neutrally with an open mind until they exhibit their fundamental style, not with a set of assumptions.
- Stay nimble even when there is indication of what you believe is their style.
- See things from different perspectives.
- Adapt and think quickly to respond to sudden changes.
- Solve problems in new ways.
- Persist in the face of difficulties and tolerate uncertainty.

Be actively flexible and spontaneously adaptive.

Obviously, the factors that persuade different customers are many and complex. Customers are different in age and intelligence, shape and size, color and gender. That is when we just look at them. They are even more different in thoughts and experiences, reactions and responses, feelings and emotions. Make no mistake of using the same approach with different customers, and do not get wrapped up in the "canned" presentation. Identify customers' needs and be flexible.

Chapter 5: Rules of Persuasion

Flexible salespeople do not:

- Force a "dynamic personality" onto a customer who is cool, distant, or removed.
- Act distant and cool with a customer who is warm, engaging, and interested in interaction.
- Talk constantly to a quiet or reserved customer.

Ability to observe and analyze customers and flexibility to match the delivery with customers' preferences allows customizing the approaches to customers' needs, beliefs, and styles. Concentrate not only on what you are saying, but also on the way customers want to receive the information. Through their behavior and words, customers tell us if they are outgoing or reserved, logical or emotional, direct or indirect. Also, they tell us in which way they prefer to receive information. *"That is not clear to me," "That does not ring the bell," "I cannot grasp on what you are saying."* Same thing said, but it will tell us whether we are dealing with a visual, auditory, or kinesthetic person.

- **Considering representative systems,** instead of a neutral phrase *I understand* we can use with: visual people *I see what you mean,* auditory—*I hear what you are saying,* and kinesthetic—*I get how you feel.*
- **Considering personality type,** for *Achievers* get quickly to the point, present the big picture, make them feel in control, and do not waste time with small talk; for *Thinkers* provide a

Selling Is Persuading

lot of statistics and facts, communicate the pros and cons, never try to rush; for *Belongers* describe what you offer in terms of safety and security, avoid being pushy or aggressive; for *Feelers* illustrate your point with personal experiences and stories, appeal to emotions, be future-oriented.

- **Considering needs and motives**, for people on a physiological level alleviate fears, on safety level emphasize security, on social level make them feel pride, and on esteem level make them feel achieved.

Too many sales have gone the wrong way because of mismatch of how we presented a message and should have presented. Salespeople have to be ready, willing, and able to reframe their persuasion efforts. There are times or situations where certain principles or tools are inappropriate or ineffective. Substitute them for something more appropriate. If logic doesn't work, try emotion; if emphasizing innovations doesn't work, accent traditions, etc. Adaptive selling is the only one based on the actual psychological makeup of customers. By increasing flexibility we can become better listeners, keener observers, and more effective persuaders.

Persuasion attempts to alter someone else's behavior. In reality, the only behavior people can alter *directly* is their own. Although changing our own behavior is perhaps the

Chapter 5: Rules of Persuasion

most difficult part of being an effective persuader, without flexibility there is no persuasion. Success or failure of your effort to influence people is determined, largely, by how well we can alter our own behavior. You can hit a home run almost every time if you can alter your own preferred style to suit that of your customers.

If our customers become more resistant or defensive, or have said nothing for a time, it's a sign *we* need to change *our* behavior and *our* approach. If what we are doing isn't working, it is time to stop and do something—almost anything—different, or do nothing. If customers tell or more often signal with non-verbal cues like a confused expression or shaking of the head we guessed incorrectly, we need stop immediately, admit a mistake, get back to the last point of agreement, and use another approach. Blaming customers for the problems we have leading them will only exacerbate the problems.

Modifying our style and acting differently does not mean concealing who we are; it just shows we are sensitive to others and flexible. It will, at least subconsciously, be noticed and appreciated. Don't fear the word acting. We all must act, and act well, to be persuasive. Acting is simply being self at our best.

There are no resistant customers, only inflexible salespeople. To paraphrase the words of Albert Camus: "Blessed are the hearts that can bend; they shall never be broken," we can say, "Blessed are the flexible; they shall never be broken."

It is the person with the most flexibility, not necessarily with the most power, who is in control.

To acquire and increase mental flexibility, like physical flexibility, requires practice.

The Third Rule of Persuasion

Newton's third law of motion states: *for every action there is an equal and opposite reaction.* We can apply this not only to the physical, but to psychological forces. The Third Rule of Persuasion is: *When we push, rather than convince, people into action, their natural reaction is to push back; the harder we push, the harder they push back.*

Resistance to persuasion is familiar to anyone who has ever delivered a sales pitch. It can be seen in a stare of inattention, a smirk, or a sentence that begins, "Well, perhaps, but…" It took me a long time to accept that resistance to persuasion is actually a good thing. But I discovered that to be persuaded, it is necessary that prospects go through the stage of resistance. If there were no resistance, we would not need persuasion. Persuasion and resistance are opposing yet integral parts of the process.

Looking for resistance, first we need to identify people whom we need not persuade: the ones who agree with us do not resist and the ones who indifferent are not persuadable. Try to persuade a person to buy a house, for example, if they do not need and want buy one. One has to be interested to be persuaded. Lack of interest means lines of communication are slammed shut and a lack of objections suggest there is no gap to fill in. We can only persuade people who have a need but not sure that what we offer is the best solution to their needs.

Whenever we try to get people to think, feel, or do something they might not otherwise think, feel, or do, we are persuading them. Having to give up their viewpoint, unsurprisingly, results in pushing back even before persuasion begins. There is no persuasion without resistance, as there is no motion without friction. Resistance lies in wait—ready if needed—and partners in a tug-of-war with persuasion.

Because of that it is important to know how to deal with resistance that can come in opposition to:

1. The persuasion process itself. In effect it says, "Stop pushing me."

2. An offer. It says, "I am not sure this is the best choice for me."

3. Change. It says, "I like the way it is.'"

So, excluding people who agree with us and those who are indifferent to our arguments, we *are* looking for resistance to persuasion. The best prospects object. Although resistance is a negative response, it is a sign of some interest indicating there are doubts in customers' minds and the lines of communication are still open. Resistance by objecting means they are considering our position and not very comfortable with their own. Objections are opinions and, therefore, it is possible to lessen resistance because it is often based on preconceived notions that are inaccurate.

Objectors allow us to show we consider their objections and feelings as equal to our own and encourage them to open their minds to our arguments. Never react to objections so it offends customers. Don't tell customers they are wrong, and avoid arguments. Instead tell them, *"Your objections and questions are challenging, sharp, and right to the point. I am sure that together we can find answers and solutions."*

When customers object, it creates the opportunity to bring objections into daylight. Resistance often consists of two parts—rational and irrational. Brought from the dark interior of customers' minds, the rational part will strengthen and the irrational part will, usually, fade away.

Find a real reason a person objects. In the words of J. Pierpont Morgan *"A man generally has two reasons for doing a thing—one that sounds good, and a real one."* After receiving a good explanation, ask "In addition to that, isn't there some other reason…?"

Although resistance is a natural part of the process, we want to reduce it as much as possible by finding ways to avert, remove, or redirect it. As there are many methods to reduce friction, so there are many ways to reduce resistance and, eventually, change it into assistance.

The following Aesop's fable shows that people understood this long before it had some scientific backing.

Chapter 5: Rules of Persuasion

The Wind and the Sun were disputing which was the stronger. Suddenly they saw a traveler coming. The Sun said: "I see the way to decide our dispute. Whichever of us can cause the traveler to take off his cloak shall be regarded as the stronger, you begin." So the Sun retired behind a cloud and the Wind blew as hard as it could upon the traveler. But the harder it blew the more closely did the traveler wrap his cloak round him, till at last the Wind had to give up in despair. Then the Sun came out and shone in all its glory upon the traveler, who soon discovered it too hot to walk with his cloak on.

Persuasion has to diffuse friction by getting the customers to agree that their and our purposes are similar and there are no reasons to resist. Figuratively speaking, persuasion has to make people want to take the cloak off voluntarily. Unless customers lower defenses and let us in, we cannot move forward and close the sale. Break resistance without fighting.

Reasons for resistance are many: justification of a position, attachment to the familiar, commitment to status quo, preservation of good judgment, etc. For all these reasons, it is easier for customers to take a stand than to understand, and to say "no" rather than "yes." It would be wonderful, although boring, if customers always agreed with us. They are not, and we need to learn to overcome their resistance.

Selling Is Persuading

Different techniques and tactics could lessen and manage resistance:

- Asking questions
- Exposing problems
- Reframing suggestions
- Proposing solutions
- Letting people retreat without losing face

To lessen resistance and to lead a customer to the desired outcome, persuasion has to do the following things:

1. **Alleviate the fear and provide the level of comfort necessary to take the risk of deciding.**

   Some people are risk takers, the majority are not. In our culture, being risk averse is not popular. People often talk brave and don't want to acknowledge, even to themselves, that they prefer not taking risks and that they crave security. Although it's a contradiction, but it underscores the problem: *Practically every customer wants something new that worked well.*

   Give customers more reassurances; providing reassurances is a form of persuasion because by allaying customers' anxiety we may change their thoughts, feelings and, eventually, actions so they voluntarily do what we want them to

Chapter 5: Rules of Persuasion

do. To lessen resistance, we need to know not only how to persuade but also how to reassure.

2. **Give customers choices that enable them to make their own decision.**

   Resistance is often caused by threats to freedom of choice. Therefore, people reject a prescribed choice, and what even worse they choose something undesirable. Persuasion begins with understanding that customers can refuse us. After all, in the process, it's the customer who must change attitudes, decide, and take actions. They feel the need to have the freedom to choose. When we give people choices, they feel in control—and that makes them feel good. So, remind them often that they have a choice. Simply tell them, *"I am suggesting the following, but you are free to choose."* Presenting limited choices will guide customers' thoughts away from undesirable alternatives: *"It seems to me that there are really only the following choices."* I heard a story about a business owner inviting a consultant to help increase sales. After observing the clerk asking customers "egg or no egg?" he suggested to change the question to "one egg or two?" The sales of eggs doubled.

   On a flight, I heard a dialog:

Selling Is Persuading

"One coffee, please."

"Yes, one coffee. And…?"

The trick is to give customers choices which we can live with and that will satisfy their wants and needs.

3. **Create a positive momentum**

   Once customers nod "yes" they will likely continue to nod "yes." A cardinal rule in sales is to avoid questions and requests that may cause the answer "no." Creating defensiveness is to be avoided at all costs. When persuading, never allow a sale to deteriorate into a win-lose contest with the customers. Do not argue unimportant issues. That will make customers feel like losers and they will be in resisting mode when time comes to discuss important ones. To be persuasive create a win-win situation, or even better allow customer to win. Be compliant on minor points. Smart persuaders understand that they need not win every battle to win the war.

4. **Move gradually**

   It is usually easier to persuade when people need not make drastic changes in their thinking. Rapid change could be unsettling. In time of constant changes, the opposing forces

Chapter 5: Rules of Persuasion

of resistance and propulsion are at work. Applying the least necessary force, we make customers feel they have decided everything by themselves and alleviate their fear of making a wrong decision. A direct frontal attack on customers' opinion awakens and reinforces the defense mechanisms. The most effective way to circumvent psychological resistance is to begin demands so gradually there is nothing to resist. Persuasion is more easily accomplished by a side attack.

5. **Express sympathetic understanding of customers' points of view and feelings**

   That is how dealing with the resistance should start. Putting ourselves in customers' shoes by asking ourselves how we would feel if someone told us the same thing can help us to say things that will reduce resistance and increase cooperation.

Let us look at how we can reduce resistance and turn things around without making customers feel bad by the **"Feel, Felt, Found"** technique. It resolves objections with empathy and understanding.

For example, a prospective buyer says, *"The price is way too high."* If we argue, prospects have a personal stake to prove us wrong. Instead we say, *"I understand how you **feel** about the *price. Many people have **felt** the same way as you do when they first heard the price. However, when they saw all of what this house has to offer, they **found** that this is the best house in the marketplace."* This technique works because it shows empathy—*understand how you feel;* lets them know that they not alone—*felt the same way,* and allows them to save face—*they found.*

For a greater effect, we can change the wording if we know the prospect's representational system. For kinesthetic people, the wording is perfect. With visual customers we can substitute *feel, felt, found* with visual words. "I *see your point of view.* Other customers *viewed* a similar situation the same way until they *saw* that…" With auditory customers, we may say "I *hear what you are saying.* Other customers *told* the same thing until they *heard* that…"

To sum it up: To persuade, a force has to be exerted by the persuader. Observation and flexibility let the persuader generate this force from within the customer reducing or altogether eliminating resistance. There is a link between what and how we say it and responses we get from our customers. By mastering the rules of persuasion we will acquire more control over responses we have from our customers, and can tap into full power of persuasion. The better we understand these rules, the more effectively we can apply them to changing customers' minds in our favor and provide them with a fair deal.

Chapter 5: Rules of Persuasion

These rules can work for us immediately, telling us what to do to persuade every customer in every situation. However, they are just intellectual exercises unless we apply them in the field. If we internalize the three rules of persuasion and keep practicing them daily applying different tools and using proper words, we will enhance our ability to persuade and lead customers to a mutually beneficial decision.

CHAPTER 6

Principles of Persuasion

"Life happens too fast for you to ever think about it."

— KURT VONNEGUT

Push the Right Buttons

Nowadays, because of exploding technology and resources, people have to adjust the way they decide. The ability to process facts needed for the right decision becomes inadequate because of all the information the modern life provides. Although we, as specie, have thinking advantage that made us the dominant life form, we have thinking capacity limitations, too. If we carefully considered every single decision and analyze every person and every situation, we would always be overwhelmed. The modern life, of our own making, often deprives us of carefully weighing pros and cons and even forces us to make many decisions automatically by using shortcuts. To survive, our coping mechanism makes us often choose with our instincts.

Selling Is Persuading

We are forced to use shortcuts. People love shortcuts to thinking because most times they work.

Shortcuts, sound rules of thumb, allow deciding on a single piece of information—a trigger. Reacting automatically to a trigger saves time, energy, and mental capacity. Minds are programmed with triggers.

Here are a few examples of shortcuts:

- More people buy Toyotas, it must be a high-quality car.
- It's difficult to find this product, it must be good.
- This guy seems knowledgeable and I like him, I will buy from him.
- This gal provided me with a free market analysis and always returned my calls; I will list my house with her.

Customers do not have time or desire to do the job of filtering, analyzing, and integrating what relates to their situation. That is where salespeople come in. They can do the job for customers and provide this single piece of information that pushes the right button spurring people to act.

Salespeople who play fairly and help customers decide by using one or another trigger will succeed more often.

When we trigger customer's highly predictable response, we are directing (not manipulating) an action that will benefit

Chapter 6: Principles of Persuasion

all involved. Only when the information is false, unethical salespeople try to exploit these triggers and people's shortcut response to them by tricking them into a decision that will benefit only the salespeople. That is why, trust between salespeople and customers helps tremendously. When rapport is established and customers trust us, we could likely trigger a shortcut.

Knowledge of the psychological principles behind the triggers allows salespeople to develop an arsenal of techniques that help customers to decide. A principle, unlike a technique, is something that is universal in its application. If a technique explains what and how to do, principle is the foundation upon which a specific technique is based. It is also behind of why the technique works.

The following principles, described by the renowned psychologist Robert Cialdini, because they are the most reliable and most of the time correct, are employed when people cannot weigh all the pros and cons when deciding:

1. Reciprocity
2. Consistency
3. Likeability
4. Scarcity
5. Conformity
6. Authority
7. Perceptual contrast

Each principle works better depending on conditions and personality types. Each can be used for having people to agree with our requests and trigger the desired action.

Reciprocity Principle

This principle states that when we give away something of *perceived* value to customers, they feel compelled to do likewise. So, they return gifts for gifts, favors for favors, concessions for concessions, and so on.

It is unnecessary to give something of material value. Smile at people, and most will smile back at you; say something offensive to people, and most likely the same will be returned to you. Give them psychological value like trust, respect, and attention, and they will usually be compelled to return in kind. This exchange of value usually works on a subconscious level.

Merely feeling indebted can create discomfort enough to want to reciprocate. The drive to alleviate these feelings is so powerful and overwhelming that people exceed the initial favor. A Japanese proverb says that nothing is more costly than something given free.

Returning a favor rids people of the obligation created by that favor. Often they say yes to those they owe. We can leverage reciprocity disproportionally in our favor by providing small gestures of consideration to others.

People give back the same feelings and attitudes we give them because they are trained from childhood to reciprocate

Chapter 6: Principles of Persuasion

or suffer social disapproval. Accepting something without attempting to give back is viewed as selfish, heartless, or greedy. Not to do it would risk being called a stealer, a taker, or a user—labels everyone wants to avoid. Grocery stores, for example, know that it is hard to take a free sample and then walk away without, at least, asking a question. Reciprocity seems to be a part of upbringing in every society. It is hardwired into our evolutionary DNA.

Because reciprocity is imbedded in most people, it is better to provide gifts, favors, and concessions before than after the action has been taken (a purchase made, contract signed, or agreement reached). A customer should be more willing to comply with a request from a salesperson that has provided a favor or a concession. Salespeople may conscientiously trigger feelings of indebtedness and obligation in customers by carrying out an uninvited favor. That's why, for example, in real estate we offer a free market analysis, a moving kit, or an "Open House" sign. While appearing to have only the intention to help, they release the natural desire to reciprocate.

Taking a customer out to a dinner, show, or sport event or offering refreshments (water, coffee, or candy) are other examples of using this principle in sales. When we employ this principle, we are treating customers as special people and building a greater sense of obligation. To implement this principle, what we have to do only is to create an obligation in customers' minds by what we do, say, or give: a favor, service, compliment, attention, smile, or gift. Any of them work if they are perceived as unselfish. Otherwise, the reciprocity principle can backfire. Manipulation is a flip side of reciprocity.

Consistency Principle

The consistency principle states that when customers take a position, they tend to defend it regardless of its accuracy. Usually a person and people around that person are better off if the person acts consistently with expressed decisions and actions already taken. Societies benefit when people act consistently and encourage them to do so. Consistency in one's thoughts, words, and actions is normally associated with intellectual strength and highly valued.

The automatic consistency has another benefit. Once people have decided, it gives them a shortcut through complexities of modern life by allowing them not to think about the issue anymore. Most people cannot hold opposing thoughts in their mind, and steadiness simply allows them to choose the one they currently hold eliminating the rest. Because it is in our best interest to be consistent, usually, we are automatically being consistent.

On the other hand, people who act inconsistently are seen as confused and insincere. People do not want to appear flip-floppers if they change their mind easily, and they like to be thought decisive when they hold the line. Inconsistency

Chapter 6: Principles of Persuasion

disturbs people enough so they will often try to reduce or altogether remove the inconsistency. Therefore, after committing themselves to a position, people are more willing to comply with requests consistent with that position. The urge to be, and especially to look, consistent often makes people do things they otherwise will not do if they did not made the commitment. The more public is the commitment, the more reluctant people will be to change it. Written commitments are usually more powerful than the verbal ones.

That is why the step-by-step close, when you ask customers questions to each of which an obvious answer would be "yes," works. Once they agree, they are more likely to keep doing so. Each commitment may be small, but it adds up and leads to the final "yes." If we get our customers to make a commitment, we have put them on the way to automatic consistency. The impulse to consistency increases with commitments.

Commitments, even erroneous ones, cause people to support them. In the words of Leonardo da Vinci, *"It is easier to resist in the beginning than in the end."*

People want to be consistent and this can be used to our advantage. For example, a realtor can say, *"If I remember correctly, you said that you need a three bedroom house with open floor plan and a pool. This house has it all. Would you like to make an offer?"* It is difficult to say no because, it would mean being inconsistent.

Likeability Principle

The likeability principle states that people liked generate good feelings in others, and people who feel good are more likely to be persuaded. The more customers feel attracted to, connected to, and in rapport with salespeople, the more persuasive the salespeople become. Attraction and rapport is a predisposition to respond to a person in a positive way. It is difficult to say no to someone we like. So, our task is very simple—to have our customers like us. It pays off to be liked, and there are things we can do to be liked.

1. Because people like those who give compliments, one way to increase our likeability is to observe and discover what we can compliment customers for. It is easier to do that we may think. We all have strengths and weaknesses, and it is equally easy to find good and bad in people and let them know that we noticed something good about them. Simply telling someone we appreciate them can make them like us more and more readily comply with our request. To compliment people is a step toward persuading them. Customer's children (although not spouses), home, car, taste and the likes are good targets for compliments. Bear in mind, compliment doesn't even have to be completely true to work. But it has to be succinct, simple, and sincere.

Chapter 6: Principles of Persuasion

2. Another way to make ourselves liked is to discover what we have in common with people and let them know about it. People like those who are similar to them and grant them favorable treatment. Anytime we establish something about ourselves that our customers will identify with, we increase our persuasive powers. This holds true whether similarity occurs in opinions, personality traits, lifestyle, or communication styles in common. The tendency to like others who are similar works because it is reinforcing people's own self-concept and helps them to predict and understand others. Similarity does make a difference. It is almost always results in attraction to the persuader as a person, but doesn't always yield credibility.

3. Evidences of similarity are essential, but salespeople also should appear different in ways that make them appear more expert, better informed, and more professional than their customers. Ideally is to be both similar enough to make us one of them and different enough to project expertise. So, dress a little better than customers, put a little of professional jargon into a speech, and show off knowledge of the subject. What also gives advantage in social interactions is physical attractiveness. In one study good-looking

fundraisers for the American Heart association generated almost twice as many donations as did others. It pays for salespeople to look their best with proper grooming, make up, and clothes.

Scarcity Principle

The scarcity principle states that when people discover that something they want is limited in quantity, time, or options, they feel more attracted to it and their desire for it increases. Apparently, scarce things appear even more desirable if customers believe there is competition for them. Short supply increases the value of what we offer and drives customers into action.

This principle pertains not only to tangible things, but also to such intangible things as time, knowledge, and information.

Letting customers know there is a real possibility they will not get what they want is a great pressure point in persuasion. The power of it lies in two areas.

1. Things difficult to posses are usually better than those that are easy to acquire.
2. People hate to lose the option to have things that become scarce.

Collectors of different items from stamps to baseball cards know of the influence of scarcity in determining the value of an item.

Chapter 6: Principles of Persuasion

Make customers aware that something about the product and service is scarce. They will be compelled to act now, thinking it will be no longer available. We, salespeople, know that many customers fear the point of deciding and want time to think it over. We also know that chances are that they will not make one. By employing the Scarcity Principle, we help them decide. *"This is the only listing with a private pool and water view in that development, and it will not last."*

Let customers *perceive* a product and service as scarce, and it becomes more desirable. It is the perceived scarcity, not the real one, which counts.

Conformity Principle

The conformity, or social proof, principle states that people are more likely to agree to a proposal well received by the majority of people in their peer group. Under the conditions of uncertainty or limited information, the principle of social proof acts as powerful self-interest stimulus. The desire to make a right decision is overwhelming, but the time to weigh all pros and cons is forever diminishing. By doing what others (especially others like them) are doing, people more often than not are making the right decision. Another shortcut saves us from thinking. Therefore, there is a strong and widespread tendency to follow the crowd. Even nonconformists conform to the nonconformists' standard. We feel free to act when we see others do some things: we litter more in littered environment; we drive faster where

Selling Is Persuading

others drive faster; and we use a fork when eating a chicken where others use. And we buy what other people buy and hire people other hire.

We are social animals, and as such we need to belong. When customers think how their peers will view their purchase, the sale can be made or broken going no further.

The validation by others gives us the guide to actions. In the words of Cavett Robert, a sales trainer, *"Since 95 percent of the people are imitators and only 5 percent are initiators, people are persuaded more by actions of others than by any proof we can offer."* People want to feel like they are part of an established group that already knows where it is going. If people find discrepancy in what they do and what others do, they tend to conform to the social norm. Why do you think bartenders "salt" their tip jars with dollars to appear that everyone tips them? This principle becomes a way to save time and energy in discovering what is the right thing to do by finding what other people think is right.

As salespeople, we have to make a special point of telling that our model is the largest selling, that our company is the fastest growing, and our product outperforms the competition. This increases social proof of products and services in the minds of customers. The more people validate what we are offering, the better. The more testimonials we provide, the more effective our messages.

If our products and services are socially validated, people are most likely to buy them.

Chapter 6: Principles of Persuasion

Authority Principle

We have been raised from childhood to look to authorities for information and guidance. As children, we listened to our parents and teachers partly because we perceived them as being smart and partly because there were benefits and consequences in doing or not doing as told. As adults, there are also benefits associated with doing as told—doing so, we can quickly and effortlessly make the usually right decision. The shortcut for that principle goes like that, *"if an expert says it, it must be true."*

Authority is both real and perceived. Customers will perceive us as having more authority if we act with confidence, comfort, and certainty. To project authority salespeople can use titles, uniforms, and verbal styles to demonstrate confidence. It is beneficial to earn designations.

To be seen as authority, we can start with:

- Gaining quotes from past clients or endorsements from local celebrities. People tend to like products and services endorsed by people they respect.
- Changing our wardrobe. The uniform effect works.
- Sprinkling our language with some jargon.

Perceptual Contrast Principle

I experienced this principle in both of my occupations even before I knew of the principles of persuasion.

As a teacher, I emphasized to my students that there are both objective and subjective measurements. Temperature is an example of an objective measurement, for example, 78 degrees. Hot, cold, and warm are examples of a subjective measurement. Then I told them about an experiment I had read about. I instructed them to take three big pots and fill them with water—one with hot and one with cold water and the middle pot with equal amounts of hot and cold water. Then, put both hands in the end pots and keep them there for a few minutes, and after put them in the middle one. Finally, they should describe the water in the middle pot as being hot or cold. To their amusement, it was difficult to judge. On the one hand (no pun intended) the water seemed hot, on the other—cold. Even though both hands are in the same water, feelings in both are different.

When the measurement is subjective, prior experience shapes our perception. Same things can be made to seem different, depending on previous experience. Contrast has to do with sequencing. This principle explains how people are affected when introduced to two greatly different alternatives in succession. An object may seem heavy or light, depending on weight lifted just before. Contrasting alternatives can distort and amplify customers' perception of things.

Chapter 6: Principles of Persuasion

I have used this principle in real estate by showing a couple of "ugly" houses before showing the ones that fit my customers' preferences. Another example of a conscious use of the principle—during a presentation I discuss the competition briefly, but discuss my services at length, making them more desirable than competitors'. I recognized the same technique when a car dealer tried to sell me optional extras after we agreed on the price of the car—the cost of the options seem relatively small when compared to the cost of the car.

Without comparison and contrast the choice is *whether to buy*, with comparison the choice is *which one to buy*.

Perception depends on contrast. In the story of a blind beggar changing the sign from "Help—I am blind" to "It's a beautiful day. You can see it—I can't," moved people to empathize with the beggar by starkly comparing and contrasting their reality with his. The essential question is: "Compared to what?"

Salespeople can commission the psychological principles to achieve their goals while using so little force that customers do not feel forced. They use the force they bring forth from inside the customers by using the principles of persuasion that satisfy customers' emotional needs—need to return favor for favor, need to satisfy self-image, or need to have what is scarce. Understanding these principles will make us aware of how people are convinced without noticing that persuasion is taking place. The principles of persuasion must operate below customers' thoughts so they do not even realize we are using them.

The principles of nature, like gravity, are universal and unbreakable. If one jumps from the roof of a skyscraper, the outcome is clear and leaves no possibility learn from the experience. But the psychological and social principles like obeying the rule, for example, are not universal and are breakable. We may break these principles, suffer the consequences, and learn from our experiences, but it is much better to follow these principles. We may, for example, run a red light and get away with it. But we are much better if we follow the principles that society created for the safety and benefits of all.

For salespeople, using principles of persuasion can be very rewarding and profitable. The problem is that many are not consciously aware of them and, therefore, do not develop selling techniques based on them that elicit compliance most of the time. Many salespeople do not realize that they already instinctively use these principles in their communications with customers. To succeed on persuasion, they have to develop skills to use them consciously, consistently, and carefully. We need to cultivate the earth before we can plant our seeds. If we have not prepared the ground first by ensuring there is liking, perception of authority, social proof and so on, our seeds will fall on stony ground. People will not be properly persuaded.

Chapter 6: Principles of Persuasion

The principles of persuasion are neither moral nor immoral, neither good nor evil—they are neutral and simply are. As long as they are natural and work toward a win/win outcome, they are not manipulative.

These principles do not guarantee success, but they improve the odds of winning people over.

CHAPTER 7

Tools of Persuasion

"Men must shape his tools lest they shape him."

— ARTHUR MILLER

The Tool Kit

Whether we succeed in convincing others is hardly a matter of luck. It is a matter of recognizing that persuasion requires tools and knowledge of what tools to use—and in what order. The more persuasion tools we master, the more influential we become.

There are many tools, actually an arsenal, which can help. Learning, expending, and consciously using the whole arsenal will enhance the ability to win people over. But remember, it would be unwise to approach every customer with dozens of tools as it would be foolish to approach all customers with one tool. We have all heard a maxim: "If the only tool you have is a hammer, you tend to see every problem as a nail." Persuasion must be customized to every person and situation by using an array of tools with logical and emotional appeal.

EMOTIONAL	LOGICAL
Testimonials	Evidence
Stories	Statistics
Similes	Graphs
Metaphors	Charts
Pictures	Studies

Some salespeople hold back on using available tools and hope that the logic of their presentation will somehow prevail. When scientists used new tools, like radio telescopes, they could see things never seen, even never imagined. By mastering new tools, we could also achieve things we never imagined.

Persuasion has changed a great deal because customers have changed. They are better educated, more sophisticated, and more skeptical than ever before. But some salespeople have not caught up with the times and still using tools that should have been put to rest a long time ago. New approaches require new tools and also reshaping and sharpening the ones that were tested by time and are still relevant. As Newton's laws are behind such useful tools as pulley, inclined plane, or leverage, rules and principles of persuasion should be behind the tools used to persuade.

But no matter what tools we use, they must clearly

Chapter 7: Tools of Persuasion

present convincing reasons of how we can meet customers' needs and solve their problems. With this in mind, let us explore some important tools.

Testimonials

Major hurdles in persuading are suspicion (customers know that we benefit from sales) and sales resistance (they fear being coerced into bad decisions).

Never assume that customers believe what we say even if we ourselves do. Our beliefs mean little unless we can prove them. Customers expect us to say that our products and services are great. But they are impressed, however, by verifiable numbers that support our claims or when others say it. Valid statistics and testimonials are partially to allay suspicions, resistance, and fears.

Statistics is one form of testimony that is a numerical proof of our claim. Figures are persuasive because they seem objective and therefore reliable. But be careful with figures; although figures can fool, even fools can eventually figure. Numbers are to be credible and when possible, supported by graphs and charts.

Some sales people avoid statistics out of fear of boring customers to death. To prevent this, use as little figures as needed and immediately connect the figures to something relevant to customers. Although statistics can support everything, especially statisticians, they ought to be specific and verifiable.

Selling Is Persuading

As you can see from the chart, our company is the number one. What it means for you is that 400 agents supported by the best marketing will work for you first.

Statistics are helpful, but before people employ our services, they need real reassurances. And the good thing to do the job is a testimony from past clients. An effective testimonial applies the principle of social proof. All things being equal, we follow the people, especially the people similar to us, who had similar experiences, or the ones we want to be associated with.

What if we can reassure customers by giving objective proof from an uninvolved third party?

Testimonial is the judgment or opinion of others going through similar situation or considered experts. It is a third-party success story that tells how we helped other customers with a problem that our prospects may also have. It provides prospects with much needed reassurances they are dealing with a professional problem solvers who keep promises and delivers results.

Testimonials speak about us so we do not have. A testimonial says, *"Look, these people had a similar concern, but they went ahead anyway. They were so happy they even put it in writing."* Having the weight of other people's support reinforces the claims.

Make clients sing our praises. Would not it be great if at each meeting with prospects a satisfied client sat beside us and told them what a great job we have done and what distinguishes us? Customers see salespeople as the same until differences are pointed out. And when salespeople offer similar products or services, differences become more important.

If this is impossible, the next best thing is past clients' testimony in writing with the contact information and an invitation to call—it adds more credibility and sets us apart. With modern mobile devices we also can videotape or record their message. Say to a prospect, *"I don't expect you to just take my word for it. Look what one of my past clients said when I helped them to solve a similar situation."*

In a testimonial, satisfied clients tell about how they were concerned about something and how our products or services allayed their fear.

When I have a listing appointment with a seller of an expired listing, for example, I present them with a following testimonial.

> *To whom it may concern,*
> *We had tried to sell our house, but with no success. When the listing has expired and a lot of agents called us, Jacob stood out by being very articulate, patient, and professional. We interviewed him. From the start, we realized we made the right decision. He explained why, in his opinion, the house haven't been sold, what to do to increase its salability, and presented us with a detailed marketing plan.*

Selling Is Persuading

> *Jacob has been in touch with us as often as he promised and exceeded the number of open houses and ads he promised. During the negotiations, Jacob was a calming presence and worked hard to get the best deal for us.*
>
> *We highly recommend Jacob to anyone, especially to people with unfortunate experience with previous agents.*
>
> *Robert and Joan Schwartzman, 555-5555*

If people with no self-interest say something nice about us, it has high credibility and arouses interest in our distinctive services. Confidently show off how you helped clients to solve their problems. Being a confident self-promoter is acceptable, even necessary, in sales.

To use testimonial letters, we must have them. Work to get the best testimonials, ask for them; build a portfolio of third party testimonials. They are a powerful tool for converting prospects into customers.

The best time to ask is when people feel good about the deal, about themselves, and about us—most times it will be at closing. Whenever somebody compliments you on what you have done, casually ask them, *"Would you mind to put it in writing?"* Usually, people do not want to spend time thinking about it and would come up with an excuse that sounds like this, *"Well, I do not know exactly what to say."* To what you may respond, *"I understand that you are busy. Would you like me to draft a letter for your endorsement?"*

Chapter 7: Tools of Persuasion

Then, have a standard letter to send:

Dear Mr. and Mrs. Customer,

When presenting my services to prospective customers, testimonials from customers like you are of great help. If you had a good experience with me, it will be an honor to receive your testimonial I can use in my marketing, and it would be greatly appreciated. Here are examples of testimonials I've received from my past customers.

Sincerely,

———————

Through examples, you can help people write testimonials. You can teach them to put emotions into testimonials, so they will be more persuasive. When sending out examples, remember that a testimonial should be phrased not so it only shows benefits but mostly so it reduces a risk or neutralize a fear.

Testimonials also are good in helping to overcome objections. Help a satisfied customer answer a particular objection in their letter and use it to persuade when a similar objection comes up with a new prospect. If confronted with an objection you do not have a suitable testimonial for, get one from the next satisfied client.

A strong testimonial letter should be credible, specific, and verifiable. It should tell a before-and-after story about us and our services that create a strong desire for prospects to want to do business with us.

The last but not least benefit of testimonials is that they make people who commit themselves in writing them more loyal. When they meet someone who may use our products or services, they are more likely to mention our names.

As important as testimonials are, do not expect too much of them. Although they give customers some assurances, they are not impartial. Customers, if only on subconscious level, understand this. Testimonials must be supported and reinforced. A testimonial weaved into a credible story can make customers experience the situation and be more persuasive.

Stories

I used to think that prepared stories were cheap. I did not use them much during presentations.

Then, I read a story about a wise rabbi.

> *"Rabbi," asked a young man, "Whatever people are talking about, you always have a relevant story."*
>
> *As you can guess, the rabbi answered, "Let me tell you a story."*
>
> *"Once, a lord rode through a village and saw a wooden fence with five painted targets with an arrow exactly in the center of each of them. He wanted such a skilled man in his entourage and ordered his guards to immediately find*

Chapter 7: Tools of Persuasion

him. In a short while, they brought the village tailor."

"Tell me how you did it," asked the lord.

"I shoot the arrows and then painted the targets around them," answered the trembling tailor.

I thought, if I can bring a relevant story to a customer just as easy as the tailor brought an arrow to the target, maybe it is a good idea to have prepared stories for different occasions.

I had a positive experience with telling stories. When teaching, I continually used them. They aroused interest, made it easier for students to process information, and entertained. I recalled, particularly, one occasion when I told them a story of how Archimedes discovered what later was called Archimedes' law.

A king in his home city ordered a gold crown. When the goldsmith presented the beautiful crown, it pleased the king very much. However, one question bothered the king. He suspected that the goldsmith diluted the gold with a cheaper metal. The king asked Archimedes to clarify the question.

Archimedes pondered for days trying to answer the question, until one day, while taking a bath, he noted that his body displaced the water as he entered the tub. Suddenly he knew how to measure the gold content in the crown by measuring the amount of water the crown displaced.

Selling Is Persuading

Cheaper metals have lower density than gold. The same weight of cheaper metals would have the bigger volume than gold and therefore displace more water. Pleased, he ran naked through the streets shouting "Eureka."

Many years later at a reunion one student reminded me of the episode and told me that because of the story he still remembers the law. Students remember stories for a long time, even if they forget some of the information.

Later, in sales, I discovered that long after graduating from school, people pay more attention to and better remember and understand information presented through stories. Creative stories could be as useful in sales as they were in teaching. They could be a savvy sales tool that entertain, engage, and *sell*.

I began to seek information about storytelling, and have read everything I could find on the subject, looking for relevant stories to modify for my purposes. I became a strong believer in the power of stories as a persuasion tool because stories:

- Touch, teach, and trigger.
- Cause, challenge, and clarify.
- Inspire, invite, and inform.
- Persuade, convince, and influence.

Stories resonate because of the way human brain functions. Humans think in stories rather than in facts. Recent

Chapter 7: Tools of Persuasion

breakthroughs in neuroscience revealed that the brain is hardwired to respond to a story. The experiments found that stories that are highly engaging and properly structured—having a beginning, middle, and end—can trigger the release of a neuro-chemical that promotes connection and encourages people to feel empathy. Researchers found that when listening to a story, not only the language processing parts of the human brain are activated, but also the areas that people would use when actually experiencing the events of the story. Hearing a narrative, brains react partly as though living through the event.

Scientists demonstrated that when people hear sensory words (sparkling, pleasant, smooth), the areas of their brains that light up differ from those that are affected when they hear non-sensory words. When just hearing these words, their brains act as if they actually see the *sparkling* new car, listen to the *pleasant* sound of a new stereo system, or feel the *smoothness* of a granite countertop in a house. Narratives transport customers into other people's experiences and, in doing that, change how their brains work. Besides, people do not expect to be influenced by a story, and so do not summon the same degree of resistance.

What makes stories such a powerful persuasion tool?

Stories:
- Are not perceived as lessons. They have been with us as long as we can remember. Fairy

tales and myths, told again and again, prepare children to deal with challenges of life while entertaining them.
- Are used naturally in everyday social interactions. Customers are comfortable with them because they are learning something without realizing that they are being taught and don't notice they are being sold something. Stories tend to mold what people hear to fit their own experiences and needs.
- Are great ways to convey information because people need not work hard to understand the idea.
- Are transporting people out of the role of objector and into a role of participant. They don't merely disprove objections; they keep customers from offering objections. A story conveys nothing to question, reject, or refute. Arguing against a "real" experience of someone in a story is more difficult than arguing against a hypothetical situation.
- Are told solely to propel people into their own personal experience and make them feel a part of a common experience. But the people in the story have to be actual, honest-to-goodness people whose experiences seem to go beyond personality and speak in common voice.

Chapter 7: Tools of Persuasion

What is even better than just telling a compelling story is to get customers to actually live the story.

To do that, stories ought to be vivid, which means creating images involving senses. Tell what you see, hear, and feel. Cause the customer to feel those sensations. Rather than just describing events, learn to recreate them. Turn stories into mini performances and make them alive.

The great Russian theatrical director Stanislavski invented a system named by his name that taught actors they should not merely simulate the desired emotion but feel it themselves to convey it to their audiences. Similarly, to create an emotional appeal, we have to feel the emotion to evoke the same emotion in customers; not just tell them what to feel or what we felt. And there is no better way to accomplish this than through an emotionally charged, relevant, and polished story. Like a play, a story must have a conflict and a resolution.

Effective story is the difference between communicating and convincing, presenting and persuading, teaching and touching. Telling effective stories is difficult. The difficulty is not in telling a story per se, but in convincing customers to believe it. So, how to create an effective and believable story?

Make it:

- Simple, so people will listen to it. If a story is too complex and too logical, it may have trouble getting the hearing. Avoid telling a story that must be explained. Although a story must be simple enough for customers to follow it without difficulty, it is not just a chronicle of events and facts.

- Interesting, so people will enjoy it. No matter how interesting, a story should not be told unless it supports or illustrates a message. Save interesting but irrelevant stories for the water cooler. Famous trial lawyer Gerry Spence, who practically always makes a point with a story, says that stories that are too logical should be disposed of, stories that are deprived of feelings should be avoided, and stories that do not engage imagination should be get rid of.
- Relevant, so people will relate to and not instantly rejected it.
- Concise, charming, and compelling. Bring it to customers' level of comprehension and make it easy to identify with.
- Informing, illuminating, and inspiring. A story is a fact wrapped in an emotion.

A story we tell can be factual or fictional, but if we put names, places, and dates into it, it becomes more believable. "**John**—*one of my customers*—*from the* **Reflection subdivision** *had a similar situation about a* **year ago**. *It would be interesting for you to hear how he dealt with the problem.*"

Chapter 7: Tools of Persuasion

People do not like fact recitations; they hate generics, but will always listen to interesting and relevant stories. Would people rather listen to a list of features and benefits or feel them through an engaging story? This is a rhetorical question. Don't get me wrong; features and benefits are important, they give peoples facts. Facts tell, but stories sell because the decision to buy is based on satisfying emotions; facts are necessary to rationalize the decision after the fact. People think they are rational, but emotions are what really move them. Stories are such a rich source of powerful techniques that go beyond the mundane citing of features and benefits. An average salesperson can list features and benefits; a successful one can tell stories. A story gets around sales resistance by engaging in a narrative, not in a list of features and benefits. *"Mr. Customer, one of my clients was facing the same problem that you are facing. It will be interesting for you to hear how what we offer helped them deal with the problem similar to the one you have."* Such a phrase is much more effective than just: *"I will tell what I and my company can do for you."* It will be effective not only because it is more interesting, but because in the words of John Milton Hay, *"Who would succeed in the world should be wise in the use of his pronouns. Utter the "you" twenty times, where you once utter the "I."* A gossip speaks to you about others, a bore about himself, a brilliant persuader speaks exclusively about you.

Repeat customers' names and the pronoun "you" as often as you can. It will get their attention because the salesperson will talk about "you" and "your" problem.

Stories should be told as to benefit both—customers and us as salespeople.

For customers:

- The benefits are in a story having the capacity to clarify the obscure and simplify the complex, and, therefore, it is easier for them to digest information through a good story. Stories can be tailored to specific situation and to a personality type and the way a particular person takes the information in.
- Emotion-based stories are not only entertaining and memorable; they also speak directly to the heart. People instinctively put themselves into a well told story they are hearing. That is, for example, why they cry or laugh while watching a good movie.

For salespeople the benefits are:

- In allowing the changing of customers' minds to be quicker, by driving the message home while making it easier to understand the point.
- In establishing credibility and perception of competence.
- In overcoming objections. Whenever you hit a stumbling block, have a story about a similar

Chapter 7: Tools of Persuasion

objection. For example, when people tell that my commission is too high, I tell them the following story I have read. *A heart surgeon took his car to his mechanic. "So tell me," the mechanic says, "I've been wondering about what we both do for a living, and how much more you get paid than me. I check how it's running, open it up, fix the valves, and put it back together so it works well as new. We basically do the same job, don't we? And yet you are paid many more times what I am—how do you explain that?" The surgeon thought for a moment, and smiling gently, replied, "Try it with the engine running."* Smiling gently, I say, "Do you know all the complexities that are involved in the real estate transaction?"

Tell a story whenever there is a need to:
- Allay fear
- Change the pace
- Brag without bragging, naturally weaving into stories whatever you want your customer to know: that you are a great salesperson, family oriented, do charitable work, etc.
- Get a client to think differently

So, find and craft stories in each of the following categories.

Selling Is Persuading

1. **Introductory** stories tell customers about you, your company, and your product or service.

2. **Security** stories show customers how what you offer has given people peace of mind, emotional and financial security. They show that other people had similar fears and how they learned there no reason to worry.

3. **Attention-grabbing** stories should get people to pay attention to you and to what you offer and tell them why they should listen to you.

4. **Informational** stories should imbed the features and benefits of what you offer instead of simply listing them.

5. **Ego-enhancement** stories should show how other people respect those who use your product or service and how this increased your customers' pride and self-esteem.

6. **Financial** stories should show how what you offer will help customers make or save money.

7. **Closing** stories should summarize all the benefits of your product or service and bring the sale to a close and get the signature.

Chapter 7: Tools of Persuasion

Keep your eyes open for fresh tales and look out for relevant stories in other people's lives and careers. Build a collection of stories of how customers benefited from interacting with you and utilize them as a persuasion tool. Also, your own life and career are filled with stories to be told and will give you plenty of scenarios and characters so you can illustrate your point or message you want to send. Have at least a dozen stories in your repertoire to use in different situations with different people.

I remember my father told me a story.

He said, *"You can find a good wife in three houses; in one she is beautiful, in the second one she is rich, and in the third one she is an excellent house wife; you are very lucky if you can narrow it to two. You have to prioritize and decide what is most important to you."*

After showing a few houses, I tell this story to the buyers and apply it to the shown houses.

If you are not a natural storyteller, do not despair. Storytelling is less of a gift and more of a learned skill. Storytellers are made, not born. A skilled persuader is a skilled story teller and vice versa.

Write stories beforehand and practice them and polish the delivery like an actor does with a role. Sales and theater have something in common: they rely on scripts. The difference between them is that sales are, usually, a one man show and as such are closer to a comedy show. Comedians have scripts, but they improvise, loosely following the script. So, maybe write no story, but just tell a story many times until you can tell it well; it will improve with each telling. A great story can be developed through iterations. The story will not be the same every time you tell it. In this way, if you forget one word, your mind will not go blank.

Questions

Whenever we speak, it is to make a statement, tell a story, or ask a question. A statement often causes resistance while a question causes reassessment. The most productive utterance ends with a question mark. Why create resistance if we can ask and direct people? Good questioning technique will allow us to quantum leap our persuasive abilities to do that. Talking is a habit, asking the right question is science, asking it in a right way is an art.

A lot of power can be packed into questions. Their power is in engaging emotions and involving minds to participate in finding an answer.

For instance, in the 1980 presidential campaign Reagan asked, *"Are you better off now than you were four years ago?"* If he made a statement about economic conditions, people would receive the information passively and would not think much about it. But by asking a question, he made people think, compare, and reassess. He knew that the comparison would put the desired answer in most of the voters' minds. Good questions lead to good answers.

The primary reason for asking questions is to gather information. There is no better way to discover customers'

Chapter 7: Tools of Persuasion

needs, detect their wants, and discover their concerns. The way salespeople are trained to do it is by creating a system of gathering information that puts questions into different categories: open-ended, closed, investigative, etc. It looks a lot like a head of garlic, a system with isolated categories. But these questions do not make people thinking and seeking; they do not persuade. As we cannot build a house if our *only* tool is a hummer, we cannot persuade effectively if we ask questions *only* to gather information.

One of a favorite question I had developed not only gathers information but allows me to start a presentation on a solid fundament. After thanking people for inviting me for the interview, I ask, "Why did you invite me? What was about me that attracted you?" They will go over my strengths and the interview will begin on a positive note. Then I can embellish on those elements.

Besides collecting facts, there are other reasons to question.

Questions can:
- Guide people's thinking more persuasively than the most logical statement avoiding arguments.
- Put us in control. When asking questions, we may seem to be the passive ones. In reality, we are in command; we control the sales process through questions. (Think about doctors questioning patients, lawyers questioning witnesses, and

Selling Is Persuading

employers interviewing applicants.)
- Allow us talk less and customers talk more so they effectively persuade themselves.
- Engage customers and compel them think and answer any and every one, if not aloud, then internally.
- Help customers recognize what they need and how to get it.
- Cut resistance by bringing objections into the open.

Questions are not created equal; some are more powerful than others. *"If I could show you how I can put more money in your pocket, you would be interested, wouldn't you?"* Such questions do not persuade the sophisticated customers of today. On the contrary, they are met with resentment and often end the sale prematurely.

To persuade, along with questions that draw information ask questions that can alter customers' thought process, change their feelings, and direct their thinking along the lines you prefer. Alongside information gathering questions, learn to ask questions that going deep, not wide. This new system looks like an onion. Like peeling back a layer of an onion, we are going deeper, prompting customers to think, reassess, and make, with our help, the right decision. People's feelings, thoughts, and actions are often molded by the questions they are asked.

Chapter 7: Tools of Persuasion

1. What is your time frame?

2. That looks (sounds, feels) like it is very important to you. What makes it so important?

3. What will you do when the house is not sold by the time you have to move?

4. It seems to me that there only two options: to price the house at the market value or put it on the market at a slightly lower price to attract more buyers, don' you agree?

5. How low would you like to put it on the market for?

Questions that persuade have to:
- Lead, influence, and shape.
- Attract attention, sustain interest, and bypass distractions.
- Allow customers to speak, find their "own" answers, and make their "own" decisions.

Entering deep into customers' minds with questions, we can steer them toward the desired answers, persuade them with their own answers and emotions the questions evoke, and commandeer their thoughts. When customers discover something themselves, they are more inclined to accept new ideas. Once customers make *their* own decisions, we

Selling Is Persuading

can congratulate them on their reasoning and the ability to decide. They will feel good about themselves and toward us.

Designed to plant an idea, to lead, and to disturb and asked the right way questions can sway customers in the desired direction. *"Do you think this might be a problem?"* is more subtle and suggestive than a blunt statement *"you have a problem."*

To persuade:

1. Ask **leading** questions that guide and direct customers by planting an idea and putting the answer into their minds. These questions are easy to ask; you simply make a statement and turn it into a question.

Look at the size of the family room. Most people love big family rooms; you would probably like it too, right?

Leading questions are, in reality, an appeal for customers consider something in a way we prefer them to think. These questions give a semi-interpretation to customers.

You seem to lean toward (the following course of actions.) Am I right?

Where a blunt statement can create a road block, such questions can introduce an idea into customer's mind they can state as their own.

Word your question in the way that leads to the answer you want. How we frame a particular question can

Chapter 7: Tools of Persuasion

shift people's thinking, limit the ways they may answer, and dramatically change the outcome. It's all in how we ask. In a study subjects who were asked, *"Did you see the broken headlight?"* were almost three times more likely to answer yes than the ones who were asked, *"Did you see a broken headlight?"* That is why pollsters can elicit the desired answer by shaping it with the question asked.

Leading question does not always require a response. It is just to make customers think.

"Is there anything more important than knowing that your family is financially OK if something happened to you"? an insurance agent may ask.

"Can you imagine how much your friends will admire you when they sit in the living room of this house?" a real estate agent may ask.

Additional questions that might help lead:
What do you think about…?
Have you ever thought about…?
How do you feel about…?

When such questions are used, we influence the possibility of the planted idea to become reality,

2. Ask ***disturbing*** questions to prompt your customers think about the consequences of not taking actions, consider what you suggest, and feel how you prefer them to. They want to make the right decision and, especially, to avoid the

wrong one. Disturbing questions can arouse suspicions and put doubts in customers mind and direct emotions.

Can you imagine how you will feel if everyone in your circle but you would have...?

Ask a couple unanticipated, even irrational, questions. They may yield useful surprises. Michael Pantalon, a research scientist, wrote, "I've learned that rational questions are ineffective for motivating resistant people. Instead, I've found that irrational questions actually motivate people better." Using his approach, I developed the two question technique to use with resistant prospects during a listing interview when I feel there is nothing to lose.

Question 1. "On a scale of 1 to 10, what is the chance we can work together to sell your house?"

After receiving the answer, I ask the second unanticipated and irrational question.

Question 2. "What made you not choose a lower number?"

Explaining the reasons for choosing a particular number, prospects may reveal what they liked and did not like about the presentation, giving a chance to change their mind.

3. Ask **rhetorical** questions to have customers accept a conclusion we want them to accept. Rhetorical questions are asked to establish the

salesperson's expertise or introduce another suggestion, not to elicit and shape an answer. They are asked to make a statement disguised as a question that puts customers in a position to come (apparently by themselves) to the conclusion we want them to reach. We all know that the best answers come from inside.

Won't buying a house with a new roof save you a lot of money and headaches?

Wouldn't it be wonderful if every member of your family could have their private room and a separate place for spending time together?

What do you think would happen if we put forward such a low offer?

Such questions soften our suggestions and allow us to be more assertive without making customers feel pressured.

4. Ask *alternative* questions to encourage a decision. To get customers' cooperation, offer choices such as, *"What do you think we should do, A or B?"* Giving a customer two acceptable options, there is a good possibility that one of them is chosen. If not, these choices will direct customers thinking away from other possible alternatives. Nodding the head when asking questions helps to elicit subconscious positive

Selling Is Persuading

response. *"It seems to me that there are really only these choices...don't you agree?"*

5. Ask **assumptive** questions to get a commitment. Communicate what you want to happen so it assumes it will. These questions act if something is true, than hide it in a question. They provide prospects with answers you prefer. Because most people do not like making decisions assumptive questions subliminally help them to decide more quickly.

Which house do you like better? (Assumption: you like one of them.)
How quickly will you want to close? (Assumption: you want to close.)
How would you prefer to finance the purchase? (Assumption: you want to finance it.)

If questions are such a potent persuasion tool, why do not we all use them? Many salespeople do not like to ask such questions because they either do not know the right questions or do not know how to ask effectively. They never learned how.

In school, unfortunately, students are encouraged to learn the answers, not ask questions. It took me some times to recognize importance of encouraging students to ask

Chapter 7: Tools of Persuasion

questions. And it took a long time to recognize that although as a salesperson I must answer customers' questions, my main job is to ask questions. And it took a long time to figure out what, how, and when to ask upon what the effectiveness of questions depends. Each type of questions is more appropriate sometimes than others.

Telling is easy; asking is tough. Asking requires deliberate thought and preparation. Although preparing questions takes time, it also saves time by helping to identify a need, plant an idea, and produce the desired answer.

When persuading a customer, do not just ask questions at random. If you watch shows about lawyers, you see how important questions asked of witnesses are in leading the jury's thought process in the direction the lawyers want. They have a plan, and know what they will ask before they start the questioning. So prepare your questions in advance; there are a few benefits to it—first, questions will be more precise, and second, they will also allow you to concentrate on customers' answers and body language. Plan your questions to ensure the answers you want.

Although we have a plan, following the prepared questioning line strictly is not a good idea. The conversation will guide on what questions to ask, how to phrase them, and when to ask them. Building later questions from answers to the previous, we can adjust and adapt to situations and people we are trying to persuade.

After asking a question, pause for a few seconds. Asking

Selling Is Persuading

good questions is a skill that comes with an accompanying skill of listening. Silence can yield important answers. Silence need to follow your questions to allow customers to consider them. Persuasion, in the end, happens in customers' minds. When they pause, wait a few seconds before asking a question. Silence breeds information. Besides avoiding the risk of interrupting, there are a couple additional benefits to pausing; by pausing we convey to the customers we carefully considering what they said and we understand the answers more than we would if we replied immediately.

Remember that right questions beget right answers, and right answers lead customers in the right direction to the right solutions. Master the art and science of asking questions.

To be useful, questions should be worded in a way that facilitates our efforts. For example, while persuading, don't ask, *"Can you afford it?"* Instead ask, *"Is this what you'd like to consider at this time?"*

Just rephrasing a question makes people feel good instead of bad. *"Do you know about...?"* And nobody feels good acknowledging that they do not. *"Are you familiar with...?"* And nobody feels bad acknowledging that they are not. Do not ask *"Do you understand?"* because customers are forced to say "yes" otherwise they will look stupid. Instead ask *"Am I making myself clear?"* And while people feel bad acknowledging that they do not understand, nobody feels bad about you not making yourself clear.

Chapter 7: Tools of Persuasion

Props

In this digital age, some sales presentations are built around technology. And while a power point presentation or a slide show can be an ideal medium with which engage larger audiences, many salespeople who sell to individuals still believe in the value of using a physical prop during sales presentation.

During the presentation, the data-collecting and fact-oriented left side of the brain needs sensory backup. Ask yourself if some element of sensory experience is missing from your message. The odds that customers will get and absorb our messages improve when we include props in the presentation. Engaging the right side brain by calling forth an image, a sound, a taste, a smell, a tactile feeling adds extra impact to our words and enhances the persuasion effort.

Because about 75 percent of information comes to people visually, and for the same amount of people sight is the main sense they receive information through, visuals props are the most effective. Visual illustrations come in many forms that include charts, slides, computer generated images, samples, and brochures. On a listing presentation, I show a brochure that I have created to show how I would promote the listing. For some people, it is easier to process information through tactile feelings or sounds, so I offer them to hold the brochure and explain with words what it would do to sell the house. Listening carefully to the words people use will give us clues to how they primarily process the information. If it is not readily apparent which sense a person prefers, use trial-and-error approach, starting with visual props. For kinesthetic people, let them touch a brochure or a sample or feel the texture of the wall or the fabric of a car seat to supplement visual information. For auditory people, slam the doors, start the engine, use music.

Props:
- Take customers out of the familiar and sometimes boring presentation format into another type of experience.
- Capture and keep the customers' attention and sharpen interest with design and color. Our messages and props share customers' attention. Coordinate messages and props so as not to overkill a useful tool. They are to support our messages and not to compete with them.
- Deeply affect feelings in ways that words can't, and can "speak" on their own.
- Facilitate the persuasion effort by making messages succinct and clear, accurate and memorable, participatory and emotional.
- Involve and help transform a monologue into a dialogue.

Chapter 7: Tools of Persuasion

When using props, you can:

1. Show and simultaneously tell to clarify it. Using other available sounds (starting the engine by a car salesman, slamming the door by a realtor) involve the sense of hearing important for auditory people. Persuading is much quicker and convincing for them with simultaneous talking.

2. Show and *not* tell when it can be enough by itself. To control where customers are looking, you may use a pen to point and, if needed, put into words what they see.

3. Show and *then* tell to capture interest.

Mental Ownership

Stories let customers share past experiences of others. But real test drives, like car salespeople do, are even better, because they let customers have personal experiences. Personal experience is the most credible and memorable factor in persuading, most likely followed by a relevant story, then a testimonial. They are more effective because they project customers into the future, allowing them to experience what it will be like to own the product or work with the salesperson.

The overriding goal of the test drive is to build "mental ownership." Psychological ownership is a potent tool

Selling Is Persuading

because when people use something, they probably will continue. Car salespeople literally take customers for a test drive, realtors may sit customers on a couch and let them see where they will put their furniture, pet shops allow them to have a puppy overnight, art galleries let them hang a picture for a while, and some companies give them free samples. I once received unsolicited Wall Street Journal for a month. And when afterwards I received a letter with a discount subscription offer, it was tempting.

If you are offering a service and can't give customers a real test drive, help them visualize how what you offer will fulfill their needs. Give them something tangible, like a brochure, to evaluate. If in your story you can vividly describe images and emotions so people can visualize what it would be like to work with you, it'll work for the same reason the real test drive works. Visualization is a form of persuasion. Create imaginary experiences: *"Suppose we agree to…, let's assume…"* Those experiences involve customers and involvement is the beginning of persuasion.

No one tool works in every situation. Pick and choose the right one. The right tools used at the right time make sure that the persuasion exerted is not very different from the persuasion accepted, or accomplished. Be intuitive. Besides the tools we discussed above, you can expand your arsenal with tools that fit you. The gravest mistake salespeople can make is to use the same tool with different customers, concentrating too much on the information presented and

Chapter 7: Tools of Persuasion

not enough on the way the information is presented. We must not only master all tools, but also be ready to use tools best suited for any situation and customer. Many sales have gone wrong not because of the facts, but because of the mismatch in how they presented information and should have presented. The best persuasive tool can backfire if we misidentify the person, deploy the tool at a wrong time, or use the wrong words.

CHAPTER 8

Words of Persuasion

"He who wants to persuade should put his trust not in the right argument, but in the right word."

— JOSEPH CONRAD

Words Matter

Persuasion is done by words. Words may be the difference between being good and being great at selling products and services, skills and ideas, talents and personalities.

Often, when selling, people are unaware of the significance of their words and the impact they have on those they want to persuade. Directly or indirectly, consciously or subconsciously, words, especially the ones loaded with emotions, have a powerful effect. Power of words, not words of power, can generate positive feelings that influence the decision-making process.

With sales, we sell feelings, not products and services. The ability to evoke feelings gives power to words. Sensory

Selling Is Persuading

words, because they make people see, hear, and feel something, are the ones that capable of stirring emotions. They make people laugh and cry, they stifle indecision and cause them to act or not act, and they sway the adamant prospects and convert them into loyal clients.

Words can affect feelings by minimizing or maximizing, revealing or concealing, and making things seem good, bad, or neutral. They can play up the positive and play down the negative.

To do that we can use:

- *Repetition* of good points by repeating and repackaging
- *Association* by linking what we offer to something already loved
- *Composition* by arranging words for maximum impact
- *Omission* of information that does not support our message
- *Diversion* by shifting attention away from undesirable points
- *Confusion* by making things difficult to understand

Besides changing feelings, words make a difference in the way things are perceived. "*Can you afford it?*" and "*What is your budget?*" not only elicits different feelings but also

Chapter 8: Words of Persuasion

brings different perspective. Because perception is the end result of communication and becomes reality in people's minds, be deliberate when using words and putting them into sentences.

Words may be similar in meaning but different in feelings that accompany them, carrying emotional meaning beyond their literal one. Most words have two dimensions: denotation—the dictionary meaning of a word, and connotation—the shades of meaning that envelop the word.

Consider these pairs:
1. *Spend—invest*
2. *Cheap—inexpensive*
3. *Sign—approve*
4. *Deal—transaction*
5. *Problem—opportunity*
6. *Try—do*

Let us look at the *sign—approve* pair. Signing is, often subconsciously, associated with signing away something. Approving is much more like agreeing. Another pair: *spend—invest*. Spending infer giving something up. Investing implies a return.

Many things could be said about a person, idea, or action; moreover, they can be said using different words. Simply by changing the words we use, we can change people's perspective, feelings, and the mental state that goes with them.

Selling Is Persuading

Look how effectively smart politicians use emotional language to influence listeners. Ronald Reagan had great success to prove his point by involving emotions. Let's take a quote from one of his speeches: *"Mr. Gorbachev, tear down this wall."* If he would ask a speech writer to write the same message, it might sound like this: *"An immediate action has to be taken to end the separation of Berlin."* The first message is emotional, specific, and it phrased as an order or request. Such a message is powerful and memorable.

Certain words have been proven to be more effective at persuasion than others. Researchers came up with a list of the most persuasive words: *discovery, easy, guarantee, health, love, money, new, free, proven, results, safety, save, and you.* These words become even more powerful when you stack them into a sentence. *It's scientifically **proven** these **easy** to use words get **results**.* Despite being used time and again, they continue to work; so, commit yourself to working the right words into your vocabulary. Limited vocabulary limits success and income.

Choosing the right words is essential to persuasion. The right words appeal to logic and emotions and create an atmosphere of trust, acceptance, and respect. They are concrete, alive, and captivating; the wrong ones are abstract, dead, and devastating.

The right word for any situation meets three criteria. It has to:

- Be contemporary, not too technical, and simple.

Chapter 8: Words of Persuasion

- Although jargon helps to emphasize expertise, it should be used sparingly.
- Be appropriate to the occasion and the customer.
- Make people feel like you are talking to them in their language. Listen, notice how they talk, then try to talk just a notch above their level of sophistication.
- Say what you mean.
- Choose precise words. Like houses are held up by what is between the bricks rather than by the bricks themselves, so meaning depends on context in which words are used. Look at this quote from theologian Chesterton, *"The word good has many meanings. For example, if a man were to shoot his grandmother at a range of 500 yards, I should call him a good shot, but not a good man."*

Understanding the words we use and reaction they cause, we will be careful when choosing them.

Choose Words Wisely

We are careful about what we put into our mouths. It is also important to be careful about what comes out. Before letting words out, think of how customers perceive them and of the image you wish to paint. *Inexpensive* sounds more professional than *cheap*.

Selling Is Persuading

Sales are lost because the words used by salespeople have a different meaning to customers. How customers perceive our words is, at least, as important as how we perceive them. Ensure that the true meaning of words is heard as intended.

Let us say, a realtor states, *"This house is a wise investment."* To which a customer may reply, *"Yes, in a few years it will be worth more."* But if a car salesperson, says, *"This car is a wise investment,"*—meaning low maintenance and running costs—customer may reply, *"You mean it will be worth more in the future?"* Our efforts will be useless if we are not clearly understood. In persuasion, clarity is of prime importance.

As a salesperson, be wary of words that muddle the meaning of what you want to say.

*A realtor is taking an old lady to preview properties. During the small talk, the old lady glances surreptitiously at a brown paper bag on the front seat of the car between them. "If you are wandering what's in the bag," the realtor says, "It's a bottle of wine. I got it **for** my husband." The old lady is silent for a while, nods several times and says, "Good trade."*

It is not what we say, it is what customers hear. Even such a simple word as **"for"** could mean "trade for" or "intended for." Meaning of words depends on customers' perceptions which supersedes whatever we might think the word means.

Taking the time to choose the right word to say what we mean goes a long way toward clarity. Avoid words that might force customers to reach for the dictionary. We do not want to appear arrogant and imply that they are ignorant. Subconsciously, customers feel that if we persist in using words they do not understand, we do not care if they are getting our point. Chosen words must produce results.

Make Your Words Effective

The most effective words are simple and short, credible and consistent, modern and moving, and last but not least—emotional. To be effective at persuasion consider the following when choosing words and constructing sentences:

- **Simplicity**

    Complex words muddle the meaning, confuse, and often cause people pretend to understand. The more complex the word, the less it is effective. Simple words make complex thoughts easy. So, adjust your level of simplicity and complexity. For example, instead of using words like *prior* and *subsequent*, use words *before* and *after*. Before and after are easier concepts to understand. Use *help* instead of *assistance*, *did* instead of *accomplished*, *use* instead of *utilize*, *begin* instead of *commence*, *see* instead of *observe*, *go* instead of *proceed*, *find* instead of *locate*.

- **Brevity**

    Never use two words where one is sufficient, and never use a paragraph where a sentence will do. More words are not necessarily more persuasion. It is not in the number of words we say, but in the number of words that customers understand and feel comfortable with.

- **Credibility**

    Credible words not only tell people who we are and what we do, but also convey that we will do what we promised. *Trust, fair, quality, competency* are examples of such words. Never use the phrase "To be honest." It implies that you are not honest all the time.

- **Consistency**

    Stay on your message. Change the words, but not the message.

Research has shown the importance of the word "because" in the persuasion process. The word is so powerful because as children we were programmed to believe and accept whatever followed the word "because."

Why I have to go to bed this early?

Because I say so.

Because it's good for you.

The conditioning people received as children remains with them in adulthood. Whatever we say after "because" will be accepted more readily and presumed to be true. So,

Chapter 8: Words of Persuasion

answer every question starting with "why" with "because."

In the new century, add and incorporate the following modern and moving words into your vocabulary:

1. **Imagine**

   This word is powerful because of its ability to evoke something different for each customer. It plants an idea into customers' minds they claim as their own, and has the potential to create a personal appeal that based on the needs and wants of a particular customer. *"Imagine how secure your family will be in this neighborhood."*

2. **Innovation**

   Many people like new things, and the word invokes the excitement of change. But with the people invested in tradition even the word "new" can imply insecurity; "renew" will work much better for them. With them what start with "re"—renew, restore, reinvent—are powerful because they take the best from the past and connect it to the present and the future, and still imply action, improvement, and progress.

3. **Hassle-free**

   Customers appreciate ease and convenience so much they will pay for it.

4. **Outcome**

   Americans, being a practical people as they are, don't care too much about the process—they want results. They have little patience with "ifs," "buts," and "ands."

5. **Lifestyle**

   It is powerful because people define and aspire to their own lifestyle.

Besides knowing what words to include into your sales language, it is not less important to know which words to remove.

Words Salespeople Should Avoid

Salespeople know words can sway customers, but they do not always understand how to identify and avoid or limit the unnecessary use of what hinders the persuasion effort.

The **first** word that should be removed from salespeople's vocabulary is "but." "And" is the word that should replace "but."

Sales give us plenty of "no" responses from customers in the form of objections. There is a tendency to send "no" back to them in the form "Yes, but." "Yes, but" is a twin of "Yes, and." They may look similar, but one is evil and the other is kind. "Yes, and" carries a positive force, and the difference is that:

Chapter 8: Words of Persuasion

- "But" triggers resistance; "And" puts people in a more agreeable mode.
- "But" is destructive; "And" is constructive.
- "But" negates what has been said; "And" adds to and redirects.
- "But" communicates rejection; "And" brings people together.

"But" breaks the persuasion process. Even if your reasoning is sound, "but" touches off a negative emotional reaction from customers. It is not what customers expect and want to hear, so they resist. Use "and" as an alternative. In using the "and," we acknowledge whatever customers said. They like to be acknowledged. They hate to be ignored and rejected. Instead of saying *"Yes, but..."* say *"Yes, Mr. Customer I agree with what you said, and I'd like to add that it would help if we do it this way."*

Agreeing + "And" + Connecting phrase + Redirecting suggestion = Changing minds

The formula shows that to convince, first agree. Agreeing increases rapport and decreases resistance. "And" promotes cooperation. The connecting phrase introduces your suggestion. Such an approach may change minds. Subtly nodding your head a few times, while making a suggestion, helps to produce an agreement. Here are examples of connecting

Selling Is Persuading

phrases: *That's why; this means that; I'd like to add; I believe.*

The "yes-and" combination will introduce your viewpoint without making customers defensive and avoid disagreement that comes with the "but." With an "and," you can move them to see the situation in its proper light and bring the conversation in the desired direction. For example, when handling customers' requests to reduce commission, consider responding with *"Yes, it's a substantial expense, and I believe in the end it will save you money because...."*

With the "and," just remember to never push too fast and never ask for more than what seems reasonable.

There are occasions, when you need to negate something. In those cases "but" may be used. It does it subliminally in the mind of a customer by canceling out everything that precedes it.

What you need to negate + "But" + Substitution = Negation of what precedes the "but"

"You can make a low offer, but that means that the seller will not take your offer seriously and will not make a counter offer."

*"I agree that the house is expensive, but you'd like to own it **because** it will make a big difference for your family."*

In these cases "but" may be appropriate because it negates the "low offer" and "expensive."

Chapter 8: Words of Persuasion

Generally, make it a habit to agree with what customers say and make your point with an "and."

"I agree with you that the price seems high, and, based on what you have said, the issue for you is not the price but quality."

Beware, "but" can masquerade as "however, nonetheless, and though." Also, you can substitute "plus, also, besides" for an "and" when presenting your viewpoint.

The **second** word to remove is "why" at the beginning of a question. If you need to know "why", soften it by rephrasing the question with "what" or "how" instead. "Why" can easily be seen as accusatory and, at least on a subconscious level, make people feel attacked and put them on the defensive. "What" or "how" is not perceived as an attack.

Questions starting with "what" elicit thoughtful replies. My grandchildren taught me that "why" produces an automatic "because." So, I used "what" or "how" instead. That, at least, made my grandchildren thinking. I used that approach also in my professional life and in other areas of my life.

That's my final offer.

Why?

Because.

"What" and "how" yields a different answer that reveals the truth.

Selling Is Persuading

That's my final offer.

What are the reasons it's your final offer?

The reasons are . . .

How requires an explanation and reveals customer's thought process.

How have you come to that conclusion?

Third, limit the use of words like *try* and *if*. Statement like *"I will try"* presumes a probability of failure. Instead use statements like *"I will."* Substitute the word "if" with "when." Say *"When you approve the papers, then…"* instead of *"If you approve the papers, then…"* "If" implies that you *hope* to complete the transaction; "when," implies that you *believe* in a good outcome. While customers might not consciously pick up the difference, their subconscious mind knows that the "if" salesperson who tries to persuade is unsure, but the "when" salesperson demonstrates confidence.

Use "can" instead of "could" *(I can do it)*, and "will" instead of "would" *(I will do it)*.

Salespeople, like most people, have bad habits and unhelpful tendencies when using words. These habits can do serious damage to them. Avoid hesitant words and phrases such as "you know," "I mean," or "like;" and, of course, the ubiquitous "ummm." These interjections unintended effect make people seem less confident, and, therefore, less persuasive.

Chapter 8: Words of Persuasion

Now that we know which words to use and not use, understand that even the right ones work with and for some people and do not with or for others.

Different Language for Different People

Research shows that in almost half of the cases where a (sales)person fails to persuade others, the failure is due to miscommunication or confusion. A confused mind, usually, automatically says no. And the main reason people do not understand each other is that they speak "different" languages, even if they all sound like English.

Meeting people similar to us, we succeed at persuading them speaking the language we are comfortable with. But people prefer to receive information in different modalities. Their psychological makeup and preferred representational system make them comfortable with certain words. Choosing words with their preferences in mind and expressing the same meaning using different sensory words, we are connecting with people. Persuasion relies not only on how we send the message, but also on how the message is received.

I'll see you soon, *I'll talk to you soon*, *I'll be in touch soon*—same message, but intended for different modalities. Unless we speak "their" language and customers see themselves reflected in what we are saying, our success at persuasion will be limited. Be a chameleon; change words to more closely match the words of customers. Great persuaders are great wordsmiths.

But even when communicating in people's "own" language, we do not speak the same way with a toddler and a college graduate, with a teenager and an old person, and with a school dropout and a Ph.D. We use different vocabulary, pace, volume, etc, so each person understands the message and is positively affected by it.

Characteristics of Speech

Voice is to the ears what face is to the eyes. It can give different meaning to the same word and, therefore, can be a powerful persuasion tool. Together with facial expressions, voice is the primary conveyor of emotions and is crucial to ensuring compliance.

Speech, unlike written text, is characterized by *pace, volume, pitch, articulation, and pause*. Because these characteristics are important in persuading, we have to discover if our voices project confidence and energy or if we sound diffident and uncertain. Then we have to learn how to change them to enhance the impact of our words. Record your speech and listen to it. Which characteristics to be changed?

- **Pace**

    To communicate talking at a different speed is as difficult as to communicate walking at a different speed. Speak at the same rate as customers because people's speed of speech shows the speed at which they absorb information. When speaking quicker than customers, they may feel confused and pressured. They tend to trust soft-spoken salespeople who talk slower and give them time to digest what is said. Slowing down makes what we say clearer and we are not identified with "fast talking salespeople" image. But do not talk too slowly, not to be perceived as less confident.

- **Volume**

    Obviously, if people have to struggle to hear us, we will not be persuasive. Conversely, if we are too loud, it does not help our persuasion either. Maintain the volume at a comfortable level. Raising or lowering your voice may be used for emphasis.

- **Pitch**

    The highness and lowness of the voice is characterized by pitch. In many cultures, lower pitch is associated with strength and authority and considered more believable and sincere. Higher pitch indicates nervousness and sounds more like a question. When voices convey uncertainty or timidity, the ability to persuade decreases. Practicing to lower the voice will help to convince people. Not to sound monotone, change the pitch to emphasize and keep customers alert.

Go up at the end of the sentence for questions; go down at the end for discouraging further discussion as if there is nothing to question. Use downward inflection before hidden commands, otherwise they will sound as questions or indicate uncertainty.

- **Articulation**

It is easier to convince when people clearly understand us; that is when we clearly articulate every word. When our speech is clear, it conveys credibility and confidence. Besides, sloppy articulation implies lack of education.

- **Pause**

Besides being an art of talking, persuasion is also an art of nonverbal. The nonverbal can reinforce the verbal or nullify it. There are two things besides words themselves that are used during the presentation that greatly contribute to the persuasion effort. One is silence, the other is body language.

Look at this page. It's divided into paragraphs and forces a reader to take short breaks between them. Speak to customers also in paragraphs with short breaks between. During the pause customers have a chance to speak, show interest, and ask questions.

Chapter 8: Words of Persuasion

Conversing Without Words

To convince, we use words, but we can also persuade nonverbally, intentionally or unintentionally. Powerful feelings can be conveyed with only a glance, a nod, or a shift. Changes to our body language can enhance or decrease effectiveness of words.

Body language is the process of communicating through conscious and subconscious physical movements.

Body language vocabulary encompasses:
- Body movements
- Postures
- Space between people
- Facial expressions
- Eye movements
- Touching
- Breathing and other less noticeable physical effects such as heartbeat or perspiration
- Micro gestures (pupil contraction, eyebrows lifts, corner of the mouth twitch)

Micro gestures are small, difficult to spot, and mostly subconscious. People seldom can control them, hence their usefulness. When customers are conversing with us, they may be carefully guarding their words, but seldom are they restraining their nonverbal signals. As a result, they will alert us to their true feelings.

Selling Is Persuading

We are interpreting, consciously or subconsciously, body language of customers, and they are constantly interpreting ours. Being a good body "speaker" of nonverbal language is important to how we come across to customers. It is wise to not underestimate customers' ability to read us. Also, it is important to being a good "reader" of customers' body language to detect the unspoken messages and decipher their feelings. We have to listen not only with our ears, but with our eyes as well. We must train ourselves to interpret.

Customers' body language can also show if we are communicating our message successfully. When customers tilt the head to one side, we can be pretty sure that they are listening with interest. When nodding, it is a buying signal to keep the conversation going.

Especially important is to interpret correctly the body's negative movements:

- Head scratching—confusion
- Lip biting—anxiety
- Neck rubbing—frustration
- Chin lowering—defensiveness
- Head shaking from side to side—rejection
- Raised eyebrows—disbelief
- Rubbing eyes—irritation
- Crossed arms—defensiveness
- Scratching the nose—concealing a lie

Chapter 8: Words of Persuasion

These are the signals that we must change our presentation.

Body language is not an exact science. No single sign is as a reliable indicator as a cloudy sky is a predictor of rain. Body language depends on context, and we must be careful not to misinterpret signals.

- Rubbing eyes might indicate being tired, rather than an irritation.
- Crossed arms might be keeping warm, rather than being defensive.
- Scratching the nose might actually indicate an itch, rather than concealing a lie.

Understanding body language involves the interpretation of **several consistent signals** to support a particular conclusion.

Certain body language is the same in all people (smiling or frowning), but some is specific to a culture or ethnicity. Awareness of possible differences is especially important in today's increasingly mixed societies.

Salespeople who intuitively know how to "talk" with their body have advantage over the rest of the field. Without thinking, they smile to put people at ease, nod gently to show appreciation and understanding, and lean forward to show empathy.

Salespeople with conscious awareness of and the practiced ability to do the same will gain the same advantage. If body language feels foreign, a lot can be done to improve it—like any foreign language. We may "speak" the body language with an "accent," but people will understand us.

Body language is a powerful concept which successful salespeople understand well. So can you. Learn and get results now.

Use the Full Power of Language

Our choices of words make a language formal or colloquial, logical or emotive, rhetorical or analogous. Words not only convey information, but surprise, grab, and convince.

Languages have many devices to make persuasion more effective by maneuvering around rationality and lowering defenses. Including but not limited to analogies, these devices will persuade where mere information falls short. Persuasion is not a completely rational process, and an analogy could touch the subconscious mind in ways that rational argument never could, making a point in a single phrase.

Brevity and creativity afford great smokescreen for the nature of analogy, which is, in reality, an argument.

Analogy, one of the most powerful devices languages offer for better understanding, shows how we can use different tools in selling by connecting something new to the familiar. New bounces off the brain like a puck off the board. Analogies glue the new thing to something already accepted so it sticks. They change perspective and bias perception and decision making. As such they are shortcuts to "yes." Analogies work quickly before customers even set up defenses. Surprising analogies stick in the craw of memory. Clichés cause the listener or the reader to gloss over rather than understand what you are trying to say. Well placed analogy is revealing and compelling.

Information tells; analogy sells.

Information + Analogy = Now I Get It

Analogy works because it delivers logic and emotion in the same punch. It makes:

- Complex simple
- Unfamiliar relevant
- Abstract tangible
- Mundane memorable

Selling without analogies is like trying to race a car on gas diluted with water. Metaphors and similes are tools to draw analogies.

Metaphor is a comparison in which unlike things have something in common. It describes what a thing is like, not what a thing is. Metaphoric persuasion may help when customers are:

- Confused

    I will *navigate* you through the complex *maze* of selling a home.

Selling Is Persuading

- Stuck on objection

  Overall, we like the contract, but if this clause is a *bone in your throat*, we will negotiate it out.

- Not seeing the difference between you and competitors

  Our advertising is a *single soprano amid a choir of baritones*.

It may help when we have to:

- Drive home a point vividly and memorably

  When we determine that a buyer is concerned with safety, we may say: "Buying a house with a security system is *having a security guard on your door twenty-four hours a day.*"

- Motivate

  With our marketing plan, the sale will be a *breeze* (implies it will be easy).

- Wiggle out of a difficult situation

  The market cycle is a *pendulum*, swinging back and forth from peaks to troughs.

Simile is an analogy that links unlike things by using words "like' and "as." "*The housing market is like relationships, it is full of ups and downs.*" A metaphor does not use "like" and "as."

Chapter 8: Words of Persuasion

- On a listing appointment with owners of an expired listing complaining that the previous agent did not keep them informed, I say: *"I will be in touch every week. But if for some reason you do not hear from me once in awhile, know that I'm a lot like electricity in your house. You can't see it, but it's there; the same goes for me when you do not see me. I still run all the tasks needed to sell your house."*

- When customers ask my opinion of how much to ask for the house, I tell them I cannot determine it without market analysis. If they ask me what market analysis is, I use an analogy with a doctor. *"Just as a diagnosis would be incomplete without tests, X-rays, and MRIs, my opinion, though welcomed, will not be reliable without comparing your house to similar houses sold in recent months and the ones that currently are on the market."* Such a simile provides them not only with reference points they already understand, but also moves a salesperson into a class of professionals. Then I add *"When I complete my research, I will call you."* When I call, they usually want to know the result right away. And my answer is: *"Like a doctor, I'd like to make an appointment so we can discuss everything and come up with the right price."*

- When sellers are unreasonable about the selling price of their house, we may say: *"The housing market is like the stock market in that a home is worth what the market says it is worth."

- With a for-sale-by-owner we can use the following simile. *"Selling a house is like solving Rubik's cube. So many pieces have to fall in line, and you can waste a lot of time without solving the problem. I can save you a lot of time and money by putting all the pieces into the right place."*

- If I feel it is appropriate, I may use a humorous analogy. To a for-sale-by-owner, I may say *"Life is like a roll of toilet paper, it seems long, but most of the times you spend it on.... Do you want to waste the next six months dealing with strangers?"* Humor may disarm people and reduce resistance, increase likability and boost confidence, establish instant rapport and engender trust. However, humor must be used cautiously. Knowing when to use a joke to relieve tension is an art; and we must also be artful to bring the conversation back.

To add wisdom to words and give weight to the persuasion effort, we can use quotations, proverbs, and sayings. Well chosen quotes will elevate the message to the next level. Proverbial wisdom reflects an accumulation of human experience.

Chapter 8: Words of Persuasion

Make Written Words Persuade

In the Internet age, more than ever, there is nothing more productive than face-to-face meeting with a customer. No encounter is more interactive. But now, more persuasion will be done not in person but through the regular or electronic mail, through the web, and other means of telecommunication. We have learned how to use words in the face-to-face meetings; it is time to transfer some of this knowledge into the written communications and onto the web.

We need not reinvent the wheel; just to apply the basics of persuading face-to-face to writing, with a few adjustments and modifications. The main difference is that we do not receive immediate feedback from customers, and we would have to anticipate and address their objections.

Before engaging in written communication, ask yourself these questions:

- Are you getting attention with your opening (subject line)?
- Are you stating the problem the reader is having?
- Are you offering a solution?
- Are you asking to take actions?
- Are you considering possible objections?

With these questions in mind, create a letter that works:

Selling Is Persuading

1. Start with a single authoritative statement and dramatize the problem so the prospect can relate to it. Whether verbal or in writing, your first words are the most important for catching attention. The best opening is just a single sentence whose purpose is to urge the recipient to continue to read.

2. All you *need* to tell should go at the beginning and repeated at the end. Everything you *want* to explain goes between in short sentences and paragraphs. The reader will understand the message better. If we want to be persuasive, we need to write economically or we risk burying our argument.

3. Explain how your product and service can solve the problem the recipient has. To catch customers' eyes the body of the letter has to be organized by bullet points, fonts, or underlining.

4. Call to action and tell you will be in touch.

5. P.S. After the opening, the most important part is the postscript. Customers look to determine whether the letter pertains to their situation and after reading the opening paragraph skip to the end. So make the postscript personal, and emotional.

Chapter 8: Words of Persuasion

Dear Mr. and Mrs. Seller,

Please don't be too discouraged that your home didn't sell because I have analyzed your home's salability. If marketed correctly, <u>your home can be quickly sold and for a good price. I can help.</u>

However, if the sale is not handled expertly your property may become "stale," and the price may have to be reduced to "below market" to affect a timely sale. Obviously, this is a situation to be avoided. Contact me and I'll explain the proven strategy I use to get "expired" listings quickly sold for top market value.

Please call me at your earliest convenience so we can get things rolling and get your home sold.

Sincerely,

———————

P.S. Please think about this seriously. If you list again, doesn't it make sense to select an agent who knows the area and how to "refresh" the marketing so your home has all the appeal of a <u>brand new listing</u>?

Check the spelling, grammatical errors will spoil the intended impression of the writing.

Letters, and also written thank you notes and holiday cards, help maintain the thoughtful and personal nature of human connections. But more and more of written communications are done electronically, through email, website, and

Selling Is Persuading

blog. Email to be treated as a letter or a note sent practically at the speed of light. Like before, ask yourself what you want to achieve:

- Is it to change the recipients' thoughts?
- Is it to install a feeling?
- Is it to make them act?

Knowing what we want our customers to think, feel, and do, we almost defined our goal. First, after defining the goal, we have to grab the attention of the recipients. Without that they will not read our message. In this case, nothing else you write matters.

To create a captivating and persuasive email:

1. Start with a compelling subject line. The headline previews and promises what the message contains. Its purpose is to get the recipient to open the email. People will open emails relevant to their situation and also the ones that stir up curiosity. A subject line has to be short (not more than five words), informative, and direct. Unlike the traditional letter, in email, the subject line, not the first sentence, is arguably the most important.

2. Open your email with a greeting. Depending on the relationship with the recipient of the email,

Chapter 8: Words of Persuasion

use the first or the last name. Reading their own name, people are more likely to pay attention to the message.

3. Thank the person. If someone replied to your email, you may write, *"Thank you for getting back to me."* If you are replying to a prospect's enquiry, you may write, *"Thank you for enquiring about…"* This puts people at ease, and, shows you are courteous. If, however, it's a first email and you cannot include a "thank you," begin with stating the purpose of your email.

4. After the main text of the email, you can thank the recipient again, *"Thank you for your consideration,"* and then follow up with something like *"I look forward to hearing from you."* Then end with a closing. Something like "Sincerely" or "Best regards" is appropriate and professional. Have a professional default signature that typically includes your full name, email, phone number, and web site. If you include a picture of yourself, you can "establish" an eye contact.

5. Because now many people check their emails on the small screens of hand-held devices, keep the email or, at least, paragraphs no longer than an inch so everything can fit within one screen.

Selling Is Persuading

> Make the last sentence of a paragraph to entice to read the first one of the next.

Another way to communicate electronically with customers is through your website. Make it attractive and persuasive. On the website, beside the persuasive message, use color schemes, layouts, and particular imagery to convert visitors into customers and visits into sales. If we want visitors to take time to read our messages, make them inviting to the human eye. Make your website easy and enjoyable to read; hard to read, hard to buy. Use letters, numbers, or bullets; use indentation and short paragraphs to create more white spaces and make the message visually attractive. To speak to all modalities of your market, use not only written words, but also audio and video. And remember, the most persuasive message is emotional and concrete; the most unpersuasive is intellectual and abstract.

On the first page, seek no immediate sale, but, like in a small talk, try to establish rapport and encourage farther exploration of the website. Then use principles of persuasion, stories, and testimonials to keep them on the site, and encourage them to visit the site again. Studies have shown that having our photos on the site improves the feeling of our trust-worthiness in site visitors.

By mastering the language and using all the power it has, we can persuade with less effort and more effect. Using the language of persuasion is actually what makes us persuasive.

CHAPTER 9

Strategies and Tactics of Persuasion

"Strategy without tactics is the slowest route to victory; tactics without strategy is the noise before the defeat."

— Sun Tzu

A Strategy Is an Itinerary; Tactics Are the Legs of the Itinerary

Although both go hand-in-hand, strategy is more important than tactics because actions taken without a goal in mind hardly succeed. An excellent strategy might succeed even if the tactics are far from perfect, but excellent sales tactics with a poor strategy will cause mediocre sales. After defining a goal, first, develop a step by step plan of achieving it. Strategy is a plan; tactics are the specific steps of fulfilling the plan.

Strategy is a military term that describes a plan of achieving a goal by capitalizing on our strengths, enemy's weaknesses, and the situation. In sales it, in the simplest terms, is a general approach to achieving a particular goal that answers the question "What we are trying to accomplish?" It is an itinerary; a guide of getting from point A to point Z. There are many strategies. Just to name a few sales strategies: general marketing, entering new markets, growth, boosting repeat business, and increase online traffic.

Tactics are specific actions undertaken to carry out a strategy. They are about how we deliver specific persuasion messages to customers so they *knowingly* and *willingly* move in the direction underscored by the strategy. When the psychological profile of a person is decoded, appropriate tactics may be chosen to advance the strategy and move customers from point A to point B and eventually to, step by step, point Z. There are endless tactics to implement a particular strategy, but, in the end, strategy defines the most effective tactics that move us toward the goal. Often, when talking about marketing, salespeople reference the tactical, or action, part of the process.

Persuasion strategy takes place in stages—from *conception, to reception, to acceptance, to action.* These stages are like a chain, and the chain is as strong as its weakest link. Any strategy has to include these stages, and each stage, like each person, requires specific tactics.

Let us say our goal is to increase production by twenty five percent in one year.

Chapter 9: Strategies and Tactics of Persuasion

There are many strategies and multitude of tactics to choose from to accomplish this goal. Let us look at two strategies and corresponding tactics.

1. **A strategy to persuade more owners to list their houses.**

- **Conception** is the initial contact with home sellers.

    Corresponding tactics: to reach homeowners through phone calls, mail, email, website, and in person.

- **Reception** is making an appointment.

    Corresponding tactics: observing customers to discover relevant information, showing flexibility, establishing rapport, getting them to say "yes" to minor things and eventually to an appointment.

- **Acceptance** is delivering a successful presentation.

    Corresponding tactics: tailoring persuasive presentation according to the observed customers' personality types, sensory preferences, and motivations.

- **Action** is signing a listing agreement.

Corresponding tactics: using the right words *(approve* instead of *sign, agreement* instead of *contract)* and shutting up after asking the big question of approving the listing agreement.

2. **A strategy to generate more leads by increasing persuasion efforts online.**

    More salespeople like the immediacy and convenience of digital technology and are adopting websites and software to attract new prospects, convert them into one time customers, and, eventually, into faithful clients and referral sources.

    - **Conception** is to decide to establish a quality presence online (Facebook, Realtor.com, LinkedIn. Maintain a blog).

        Corresponding tactics: research different venues, speak with fellow salespeople about what they are doing, and look at different real estate related websites.

    - **Reception** is to join multitudes of Internet platforms.

        Corresponding tactics: decide which venues to choose and contact them to discover the cost; learn how to create a blog.

Chapter 9: Strategies and Tactics of Persuasion

- **Acceptance** is to hire professionals to help with the task.

    Corresponding tactics: research and hire professional photographers, videographers, and web designers to help to project professionalism.

- **Action** is to have everything in place by the beginning of the year and start actively using every chosen platform.

    Corresponding tactics: create a website, improve contents and looks on company's website, have a website for each property being marketed with specific web address to attract home buyers, impress home sellers, and make it easy for other agents to learn about the property. On LinkedIn, for example, update the status, share a useful post, follow new real estate pages, answer inbox messages, even it is just to say "thank you." It is easy, quick, and much appreciated. We never know where it might lead.

Different Approaches to Different Situations and People

Strategies and tactics would be easy to learn if all people reacted the same way. They do not. One of the biggest mistakes rookie salespeople make is treating all customers the same. Winning people over requires different approaches, therefore strict scripts do not work well if at all.

Selling Is Persuading

Customers rarely fall into neat little categories that allow salespeople to use a single tactic. Human behavior is too complex for cookie-cutter approaches. That is what makes persuasion challenging, but also fascinating.

Fortunately we need not start from scratch. Customers are persuaded in few predictable ways and there are approaches that are most effective for each. Once we learn to observe without premature judging, develop flexibility, and train ourselves to listen with empathy, we will discover things about people that will allow us to choose appropriate approaches. We have to have a repertoire of approaches tailored to a family, a young couple, an older couple, or a single person.

Certain persuasion tactics and tools work with some people while they are not so effective with others.

The four personality types prefer to be persuaded in different ways. In your persuading strategies and tactics focus: with Belongers on relationship and trust, with Achievers on evidence and results, with Thinkers on facts and logic, and with Feelers on vision and emotions,

Because people "view" the world through different senses, certain words work with some people and do not with others. Speak "their" language. For visual people, use tactics that show more and talk less. For auditory people, use tactics that tell more and show less. For kinesthetic people use tactics that let them touch and feel.

Chapter 9: Strategies and Tactics of Persuasion

As to people's place on the hierarchy pyramid, tactics should: on **security** level not emphasize any characteristics of what you offer that can be viewed as increasing risk, on the **belonging** level emphasize how your products and services will help them win the approval from others, on the **esteem** level, show how what they buy demonstrates their achievements.

When persuading, use strategies and tactics that do not ignore customers' need to win. Employ approaches that make them feel like winners. Every win brings pleasure. The cumulative effect of many small wins will be greater than that of one bigger because the subconscious counts every win as just a win regardless of the size. Small wins' values are psychologically inflated.

Matchers and Mismatchers

Some people are risk takers; they feel comfortable and excited moving toward something. Some people are more cautious, they move away from something they see as a threat. So, after discovering their needs and wants, the strategy is to emphasize what is relevant to how they relate to the world.

Persuasive strategies and tactics differ with people who are "matchers" or "mismatchers."

- "Matchers" look for similarities and like their world to stay the same. They will say what they

Selling Is Persuading

want in a house, a car, or any other product we sell. Selling, for example, a car to a "matcher," stress that although the car has a lot of new features, it's as reliable as the previous model, and also as easy to operate and maintain. Tell to a "matcher," *"Although it is better, it is as easy to operate and maintain; and everything you have will work with the new thing."* Explain to them how their decision will improve what they already have. To persuade them, stress that the house requires little maintenance; the car uses little gas, etc. A powerful way to persuade "matchers" is scary them by having them to imaging undesirable outcomes of rejecting your offer, and then reassure them that whatever they imagined will not happen thanks to your solution.

- "Mismatchers" like the excitement of change and look for differences. They will say what they do not want in a product. Selling to a "mismatcher," emphasize the differences: excitement of a new design, added features, etc. Talk to them about new exciting things that will happen when they buy the product. To persuade them, emphasize how big the house is, how fast is the car, etc. Motivated by what they will gain and achieve, let them imagine the consequences of failing to reach their goals.

Chapter 9: Strategies and Tactics of Persuasion

As they differ, so our strategies and tactics should be different. If we know whether our customers match or mismatch, we know what will appeal to them. To discover if a customer is a "matcher" or a "mismatcher," ask to compare two things. Usually, a "matcher" will do the comparison by finding similarities, a "mismatcher"—by emphasizing differences. "Matcher," usually, will agree with you, "mismatcher"—disagree.

Imagine you could read people's mind and be able to influence and persuade them. Imagine that you know the exact words to use with particular customers. Imagine that you know how to create impressions conducive to your persuasion strategy. Knowledge of psychology and techniques based on this knowledge can translate these dreams into reality, giving you directives on which strategies and tactics to use.

CHAPTER 10

Negotiation Is a Two-Way Persuasion

"Start out with an ideal and end up with a deal."

— KARL ALBRECHT

If Unable to Persuade, Negotiate

There are many ways to influence: coercion, order, or intimidation, just to name a few. "Unfortunately," these methods do not work for salespeople because money and power belong to buyers, and information is accessible. This leaves only two ways to get people *voluntarily* and *knowingly* do what we want them to do:

1. **Persuade**
2. **Negotiate**

Although often used interchangeably, these approaches are different.

Selling Is Persuading

- **Persuading** is convincing through reasoning and emotions to take the desired actions. Persuasion is less costly than negotiation. It is the weapon of choice. One of the reasons that persuasion fails to sway the other party is that we use arguments that sound persuasive to us, which assumes that the other party thinks the way we do. Effective persuaders try different approaches, framing their ideas and information accordingly to what they have learned about the psychological makeup of the opponents. But persuading using different approaches and getting the same response indicates persuasion has run its course and it is time to switch to negotiation.

- **Negotiating** is to reach a mutually satisfactory agreement by *trading concessions* and *persuading* opponents those concessions give them what they need if not what they asked for.

Persuasion is about talking and negotiation is about trading, but they are not mutually exclusive.

Negotiation is an interactive communication—a dialogue—that parties employ when they cannot get what they want from each other by arguments only and need to reconcile the conflicting interests with something more tangible—giving something up. Which strategy—persuasion

Chapter 10: Negotiation Is a Two-Way Persuasion

or negotiation—is best depends on the context, but skills of positive influencing should be employed in both situations. Persuasion is an essential part of negotiation; we cannot negotiate without it. But, sometimes, without concessions, persuasion alone is not enough to close the deal. Arguments and emotions plus concessions are the bread and butter of negotiations.

As there are two sides to every coin, there are also at least two sides to every negotiation—literally (there are two parties negotiating) and figuratively (negotiations involve not only heads but also hearts.) The latter means that when negotiating, we have to consider that people are not machines and are influenced not only by logic of the compromise but also by the emotions the compromise brings into being—consciously or subconsciously. Negotiation is not rocket science, but to have a sound strategy we need more than just gut feelings.

If the time comes when we can delegate negotiation to computers, it will be pure logic. But until emotions are there, they can be an asset or a liability during the negotiation facilitating achieving or destroying the possibility of an agreement, and lead more quickly to change. Emotions are contagious. When the other side becomes too emotional, rather than to react to every emotion negotiating partners have, we ought to understand what motivates them. Avoiding inflaming the situation with aggressive responses of our own, we would not come across as judgmental or critical.

Emotions are a power we can harness and use in practically every aspect of persuasion or negotiation process. Logic is to justify emotionally made decisions. Logic makes people think, emotions make them act. In negotiations, emotions are stimulated by the need of safety, appreciation, affiliation, status, esteem or lack thereof. The difference between having those needs met or ignored can be successful or failed negotiation. So, during the negotiations, freely express appreciation, acknowledge status, boost esteem, indulge ego, and increase the feeling of security. People secretly want that beside what they tell they want. And above all, make negotiation partners feel like winners.

Win-Win Versus Win-Lose

The key skill in negotiations is to fit all wants together so all involved get what they need—not necessary what they wanted when negotiation began—and make everyone feel like a winner. When we manipulate people into a deal in which they do not get what they need, we generate only remorse, resentment, and revenge. Turning negotiation into a confrontation, we lose even if we "win." Winning battles does not win wars.

To win the war, we need the other side to feel they, at least, did not lose; even better, make them think that they have won. Winning is a perception, and enhancing the perception that our opponents are winning without us making real concessions to them we can persuade them they have

Chapter 10: Negotiation Is a Two-Way Persuasion

won. Allowing the other side to prevail in a battle of our choice, we may generate good feelings that will get us closer to winning the war. It is easy to defeat someone, but hard to win someone.

To create a win-win outcome, we have to use a kind approach, a humble attitude, and careful attention to the other side's needs. If we know their needs, we can offer options that will result in a win-win. It will always carry us further in negotiation than the assumption that our needs are important and theirs are not. Start as a person, before becoming a negotiator, and view the other side as an opponent, rather than an enemy.

Negotiation, like diplomacy, is the art of disagreeing without being disagreeable and finding points of agreement.

Although parties sit on the opposite side of the table during negotiations, they will become partners when the deal is sealed. Even when you reject a proposal, do not reject the person—separate the issue from personality. Also, separate the customers from their problems. Negotiation is not over after the rejection and is easier by such a separation to resume. If you make no deal, at least build a relationship.

To have a successful negotiation, prepare for it. Preparation is too often a neglected negotiation skill. Prepare a strategy based on knowledge gained about counterparts from the beginning of the relationship:

- What personalities are we dealing with?
- What words will they respond to best?

- What are their true needs?

We have to know as much as possible not just about the object of the negotiation, but also about people we negotiating with.

Each negotiation will be different, but there are vital rules to follow to guarantee success. A little knowledge of human psychology allows predicting the other party's next move, and familiarity with the negotiation process helps to structure negotiation.

Rules of Negotiation

1. **While negotiating, ask a lot of questions.**

Within a negotiation, power goes to those who listen and learn. The one with the most information will walk away with a better deal. Give the negotiation partners the honor of talking. To obtain information, ask a lot of questions.

Benefits in asking questions:

- Questions give us time to think.
- Questions have negotiation partners see weaknesses in their position, rather than we pinpointing these weaknesses.
- Questions force the other side to speak.

After asking a question, be silent and listen. Knowing when to speak and when to be silent will give an edge in negotiation. Silence is a great tool of a skilled negotiator.

Chapter 10: Negotiation Is a Two-Way Persuasion

An effective questioner and listener have the advantage over the talker in almost every negotiation. Be comfortable with and do not underestimate the power of silence. If you are not comfortable, neither is your negotiating partner. The common result of the uncomfortable situation is that one party will break the silence with a concession. Whether it is a few seconds or a few minutes give them the honor of speaking.

2. **Know what you want and what you can live with.**

Before learning what your negotiating partner wants, know what you want. When deciding on a negotiating strategy, knowing what you want to achieve and what you can accept will help you choose the right approach. You gain a psychological edge over your negotiation partners when working toward a specific goal.

The goal in a negotiation is to get the highest reasonable outcome of what we should achieve. Having a goal as the reference point for success instead of the bottom line will focus us on the goal instead on the bottom line. The bottom line is the minimum we will accept in a negotiation. When we do not reach our goal, we still have room for negotiation. We don't have to get everything we want, just some of it. Sure, we'd like to get everything we asked for, but the world will not end if we do not. Having options means we can be flexible. Only when we cannot achieve our bottom line, we would rather wait or search for another solution.

From the beginning, we have to divide our priorities into two categories:
1. What we *must* have.
2. What we would *like* to have.

For example, when someone decides on buying a certain house, as a realtor, you can discuss what the buyers might like from the sellers if they cannot have the house for the ideal price. When representing the sellers, discuss what concessions they can make to reach the desired price. During negotiation you can buy what you need with what you would like. Give in on a few likes, and ask for concessions on what you need.

In sales, we do not get what we want,
we get what we negotiate.

Although you have goals in negotiations, it is dangerous to predetermine specific ways a negotiation will go. In a negotiation there are so many personal, situational, and unanticipated variables we ought to be prepared by playing out different scenarios. There is no script, and, anyway, the other party does not know the lines we prepared for it.

3. **Do not narrow negotiation to one issue.**

Usually the one issue is the price. But if the only thing left to negotiate is price, there is no room for a win-win outcome. Fortunately there are, usually, many more elements

Chapter 10: Negotiation Is a Two-Way Persuasion

that may be important. In real estate, we can offer or be asked for repairs, help with a down payment, or accommodate time requirements. When negotiating a car purchase, we can offer or ask for free oil change, additional features, or better financing.

Most people assume negotiation is always about money. For example, one real estate agent advises his client to make a full offer and ask for two months to close to obtain financing. The other agent asks questions and finds out that the sellers have a problem: the husband received a job offer in another state and they need to move in two weeks. This agent advises his client to offer reasonably less than the asking price, close in two weeks, and attach no contingencies. The first buyer offered more money, but the second solved the problem. If we want to pay a lower price, the other components of the offer must be as attractive as possible.

4. **Start with an extreme position**

Starting high skews the entire negotiation in our favor. The starting point often affects people and subconsciously adjusts their expectations. By asking for more, you make the request the anchoring point for future negotiations. As a rule, the more extreme the first offer, while still being reasonable, the higher is the counteroffer and the settlement price.

"*When the final result is expected to be a compromise, it is often prudent to start from an extreme position.*"
—JOHN MAYNARD KEYNES

If we do not get the desired price, then we concede to the desired outcome. We can gradually make concessions and still hit our goal. *Gradually* is the key word because granting quick concessions is perceived as a sign of weakness.

When making or asking for concessions, it helps to know the strength of the position we are in. For example, when representing a seller in selling a house, consider all the benefits the buyer will receive. Is the house convenient as to transportation? Is it in the safe neighborhood and good school district? Consider the dynamics of the market. Is it a seller's market? Is it a buyer's market? Are we pressed by a deadline, or do we have time to wait for the best offer? Deadlines greatly affect the balance of power in a negotiation. Knowing our strengths gives us power and confidence to ask the other side for more than we expect to get. As to the buyer, it is important to justify a low offer. Without justification, seller may conclude that the buyer are not dealing in good faith and refuse to negotiate. Here are examples of how to justify low opening: the house needs work, comparables are low, the schools are not the best, this all we can afford.

- Asking for more, we will probably get more. But if we don't ask for more, how likely is it we would get more? Wayne Gretsky, arguably the greatest hockey player, said: *"You lose 100% shots you do not take."*

Chapter 10: Negotiation Is a Two-Way Persuasion

- Asking for more may also be employed by our opponents. When the other side starts high, learn to create an impression they have gone too far in their request. It can be done with a raised eyebrow, a grimace, or a disbelieving gesture. Try to change the initial request; otherwise it serves as price anchor. Car dealers are notorious doing that. So being on the other side of receiving a high offer, we have to make them to reduce it immediately. We can say, "Do not be ridiculous, give a realistic offer." When they say, "It is a realistic offer," we can say, "so, this a 'realistic' counteroffer."

- Asking for more, will give us some negotiating room. The reciprocity principle works for concessions as well as for favors. By starting high that is almost always rejected and then retreating to a moderate proposal we had in mind we may reasonably expect a reciprocal concession.

- Asking for more prevents the negotiation from deadlocking. Usually, I advise sellers to ask more than they will accept and buyers to offer less than they will pay. This is basic psychology—people feel satisfied when they get concessions.

- Asking for more, we can make concessions and make the other side to feel they won. We, humans, have an innate need to save face. If we deny our negotiating partners of the opportunity to do that, they have, again, an innate desire to get even.

5. **Get the other side to make the first offer and never accept it**

If we have enough information about market value, we may open. Otherwise give the other side the honor to open. They may surprise us with low aspiration. A buyer may offer more than the seller was expecting, or a seller may accept less than the buyer would pay. Usually, who makes the first offer loses.

Even if the first offer is good, as a rule, do not accept it. Did you have an experience of the other side quickly accepting your offer without countering? How did you feel? What can be wrong in accepting if the offer is good?

A few things:

- The other side may think "We could have done better."
- They may think "something must be wrong."
- And finally, we probably have lost some concessions.

Chapter 10: Negotiation Is a Two-Way Persuasion

The result of negotiation is supposed to be more than just a deal. The offers and counteroffers, converging on a price and terms acceptable to both sides, comfort everyone that they did everything to get the best deal. Research shows that the most likely outcome in a negotiation is the midpoint between opening offers.

6. **Make concessions, but never offer to split the difference**

Negotiation is a compromise. It is about concessions that provide space to negotiate in. To know how much space, make a list, even two lists, of concessions—one of those you will make, and the other of those you are not. Concessions can be real or symbolic, tangible or intangible, monetary or non-monetary. What counts is the feeling about the concessions. People enjoy the satisfaction of telling about the "great deal" they negotiated. *What* we give up may be less important than *how* we give up.

Do not concede too early, do not make unnecessary concessions, and do not concede without gain.

After making a concession, ask for a reciprocal concession right away. Do not count on them making it up to you later. The value of a concession goes down rapidly in the other side's mind.

If we followed the first rule and asked for more, we can concede by throwing something out. Concessions give people sense of having won, and the deal looks better for the other side after something has been thrown out.

A story I heard as a child illustrates this principle.

> There was a poor family living in a small dilapidated house. Every year they had an addition to the family so that at one point the situation has become unbearable.
>
> The wife went to the rabbi, explained the situation asked for advice. The rabbi thought for a while and then said, "You have a goat, don't you? Then bring it into the house." This seemed ludicrous to the wife, but the rabbi had a reputation of a wise man so she followed his advice. The wife returned to the rabbi a few more times, pleading for help. The advice was to move in the chickens, then the dog.
>
> Finally, the wife approached the rabbi with a desperate plea, "Please, help us. We can't live like this. Children are crying, the goat is destroying the walls, and the dog is chasing the chickens, so the feathers as well as harsh words are flying around. Please, help us."
>
> This time the advice made sense to the wife. "Remove the goat from the house." After a few more visits when the rabbi asked for the removal of all animals, the wife said, "Thank you, rabbi, so much. It is now so quiet in the house, everyone is so happy."

The moral of the story is that to make the other side happy, let them throw something out. The more they can

Chapter 10: Negotiation Is a Two-Way Persuasion

throw out, the happier they are. No matter what we are negotiating, each side must be able to explain to itself and, especially, to others why the agreement was in its interest. The bigger the concession, the more important the explanations become.

In small and large things, we usually split the difference. Splitting the difference appeals to our sense of fairness, it is easy to understand and quick. Once concession is put forward—regardless of attached "ifs"—expectations are going up. Therefore it is better to wait when the other side offers to split the difference; then you know where they stand. The side that suggests split the difference in half already lost half of its negotiating power.

Sometimes, concessions produce no deal. And it may be not a bad outcome, because no deal is better than a bad deal.

In negotiations, we do not want to disclose that we have the authority to make concessions. Car salespeople are notorious about this with their famous "I have to ask my supervisor about this." As a realtor, negotiating a sale, I can tell the seller (buyer) that the price (offer) is not realistic, and that I do not have the authority to decide. I would have to consult with the principal.

When making a concession, always ask for a trade-off. When people get something for nothing, they appreciate it less, and may be inclined to ask for more. So, never make unilateral concessions. That means always attach a string to it and ask for something in return.

Selling Is Persuading

Psychologically, right after making a concession is best time to ask for one. When sellers ask me if they should fix up something before putting the house up for sale, I tell them it depends. Spending a few hundred dollars makes sense because it increases appeal of the house and, therefore, its marketability that may bring thousands of dollars more for the house. But if a major repair needed, let buyers ask for it. *"Yes, I will change the roof if you pay full price."* They would feel they won something.

> *"Power concedes nothing without a demand. It never did and it never will."*
> — FREDERIC DOUGLASS

Now that we understand the importance of concessions in the negotiation process, the question is how to make them. Concessions should not be the same size: each one should be less than the previous. Let us look at negotiating the price of a house. A buyer offers $240,000 for against the listed price of $300,000. The seller drops the price $10,000, which the buyer counters with $5,000 increase. The seller comes down another $10,000, and the process repeats itself. After a few repetitions the buyer recognizes the seller's pattern and expects another drop of $10,000. It is a bad strategy. Instead, if the seller after initial concession of $10,000 drops the price $5,000, than $2,000, the buyer will get the message of the seller's bottom line, and will likely be satisfied with the best possible deal. For negotiations to succeed both parties have to feel they are not taken advantage of.

Chapter 10: Negotiation Is a Two-Way Persuasion

Understanding how to negotiate properly will give us the power to command any situation so we can get the best deal for our clients, us, and our company.

Chapter 11

Subliminal Persuasion

> "*The conscious mind may be compared to a fountain playing in the sun and falling back into the great subterranean pool of subconscious from which it rises.*"
>
> — SIGMUND FREUD

Subconscious Mind

Even great thinkers make discoveries on a flash of intuition. Anecdotes about Newton and the apple that fell on his head and Archimedes shouting "Eureka" in his bathtub or the fact that Russian chemist Mendeleyev saw his periodic table of elements in a dream show that more goes on in people's brains than they are aware of.

People are constantly and mostly subconsciously evaluating multitude pieces of information and deciding outside of consciousness. They perceive, make judgments, and act—and in all these endeavors they are influenced by factors they are not aware of. Conscious awareness of the reality results from all the information registered and processed by the subconscious, and, therefore, what is going on in our minds is going through two parallel tiers. The staff with which persuaders work is the fabric of people's mind, and that gives us also two paths to persuasion:

1. **Conscious.**

    It is the path of deliberation and analysis. Persuade the conscious mind with evidence, statistics, and charts.

2. **Subconscious.**

    It is the path of feelings of pain and pleasure. Persuade the subconscious mind with analogies, stories, and hidden commands.

Although seemingly independent, conscious and subconscious minds are not opposite, but reluctant partners in deciding. Their tense cooperation may be captured by analogy in which the intuitive side is an untamed horse and the rational side is the jokey. To reach the goal they need to work together. To move things forward, we must work with both, remembering that it is the horse that does the work planned by the jokey. You must give the jockey the why, where, and how to move, and motivate the horse who is getting the job done. It is the jokey who resists, but what looks like resistance is often the lack of clarity. So, clear the

Chapter 11: Subliminal Persuasion

path. Direct the jockey, motivate the horse and make it easy for them to move in the desired direction.

In this partnership, the subconscious mind is the senior partner. It makes sense to work with the senior partner that exerts influence without conscious awareness to move through the cleared path. If we can, unbeknownst to people, reach their subconscious, we can influence their decisions. Appeals which motivate people are often hidden.

People are subconscious decision-makers with a touch of logic.

Scientists, until recently, and with them nonscientists, overestimated the power of the conscious part of the brain. As a result, most traditional sales techniques teach how to persuade people by influencing their conscious mind. In reality, most thoughts and emotions rest below the surface like the bottom of an iceberg, and conscious decisions have their roots in and receive instructions from below the surface subconscious mind. Knowing how the human brain works enables us to reach the elusive subconscious decision-maker. From now on, we have to focus more on the hard-to-pin-down emotional drivers of customer's decision making. It has only been in the last few decades that science shed some light on exactly how that works. New sales techniques able to access the subconscious mind based on that science are now having been developed.

Prior to the twentieth century, persuasion and brain science were different fields. Persuasion essentially was an art based on talent. During the century science established relationship between persuasion and brain. By midcentury it was strengthened, but the knot was tightened only around the turn of the century. The marriage was solidified by research on how the human brain works to influence our feelings, choices, and actions. All offspring benefited from this marriage, but especially the ones who chose the field of selling.

It's not like in the past people did not know of the subconscious. Scientists actually *speculated* about the subconscious aspects of human behavior, Freud being the most famous.

> *"There is a road from eye to the heart that does not go through the intellect."* —G.K. Chesterton

> *"The heart has its reasons of which reason knows nothing."*
> —B. Pascal

> *"The only real valuable thing is intuition."*
> —A. Einstein

Because of new discoveries, not speculations, now, we better understand the role of the subconscious. The contours of a new paradigm reveal the startling dependency of persuasion on the subconscious mind. Although important, the conscious mind is the end result of what is going on in the subconscious. Important thing to remember is that *people are persuaded by logic, but moved by emotions*; and emotions are

Chapter 11: Subliminal Persuasion

ruled by the subconscious. The obvious conclusion from this is that if you want to influence customers' decisions, you need to persuade them emotionally, not just logically.

The subconscious mind may be concealed, but its effect on the conscious decision making is not. It is independent, purposeful, and active. Combining all the information we receive, it determines what we are feeling. These feelings are influencing the conscious part in many ways: how we view people, how we make quick judgments and decisions, and what actions we undertake because of hunches we cannot explain.

The subconscious mind of a customer is the place where most decisions to buy are made.

Recent advances in neuroscience, psychology, and linguistics helped salespeople to understand the importance of influencing the subconscious mind with new techniques not seen as persuasion. Dave Lakhani who has written extensively about the subject has said, *"Persuasion that looks like persuasion isn't persuasive anymore."* These techniques are called *subliminal persuasion*. Rather than forcing someone to do certain things or think certain way, subliminal persuasion is more like a tap on a back or a nudge on a shoulder.

Engage the Subconscious

Neuroscience claims that 95 percent of decisions are made by the subconscious. Why concentrate on the 5 percent? Because much of persuasion occurs below (sub)

Selling Is Persuading

people's conscious recognition, subconscious mind is the route of least resistance in the persuasion process. It will digest what we feed it without conscious awareness. Although subliminal persuasion consists of messages that operate below the conscious awareness, it nonetheless greatly influences customers' thoughts, feelings, and acts.

Ultimately, persuasion is the ability to reach the subconscious decision-maker within a customer.

The following persuasion techniques we have discussed throughout the book, although not labeled as such, are subliminal in their nature. Their power is in convincing without customers realizing that they are being persuaded.

1. **Establishing rapport**
   Techniques used to establish rapport with customers (discussed extensively in chapter 4) are a subliminal persuasion because they affect without conscious recognition.

2. **Dressing persuasively**
   In the same chapter, we discussed the importance of dressing appropriately. When we sell the intangibles—insurance, investment, or real estate services—our attire and surroundings can send subliminal messages helping to visualize the invisible: leather briefcases symbolize prosperity, coordinated dresses, footwear, and

accessories are a sign we pay attention to details, and grand offices and luxurious cars imply success and longevity.

3. **Triggering actions**
   As life becomes busier and more complex, principles of persuasion (discussed in chapter 6) will have people follow rules of thumb that let them decide on a single trigger with little of conscious consideration.

4. **Persuading with questions**
   Carefully constructed questions (explored in chapter 7) embed themselves in the mind of a customer. This is a powerful subliminal persuasion technique because it allows hijacking and steering customers' thoughts by having automatically searching for answers.

5. **Telling stories**
   In the same chapter we discussed stories. They are so rooted in one's upbringing that for many stories act as anchors of relaxation and involvement and as such bypass conscious resistance and slip into the subconscious mind. Stories slide past the logic and engage emotions.

6. **Choosing words**

   Persuasion has a lot to do with how skillfully we use words to subliminally weave our intentions into conversation considering people's dominant sense. What words we use or not use and how we construct sentences emphasizing certain words can influence people without them realizing what is going on. This discussed in chapter 8.

7. **Using analogies**

   In the same chapter we discussed analogies that are vehicles for transporting subconscious thoughts into conscious awareness. They direct customers' attention, enable them to make sense of information, and influence their perceptions, decisions, and actions.

8. **Using logic and emotions**

   Each customer has different balance of logic and emotions. Thinkers need more logic and, therefore, we need work more on their conscious mind; Feelers require more attention to emotions and more work on the subconscious part of their mind. Rational thinking only justifies emotional choices. We have to use persuasion techniques that provide customers with

Chapter 11: Subliminal Persuasion

feelings of comfort and enthusiasm about the decision to buy and give logical reasoning to the conscious mind so it can rationalize the decision that manifests itself in a form of verbally expressed thoughts. All the right thoughts usually come after emotions caused us to act. Reasons just placate the conscious.

The following examples show how else we can influence the subconscious.

- When I secure an appointment with prospects, after some small talk, I usually thank them for the opportunity: *"Thank you for the opportunity to show you how I work."* But then I have learned to increase the effectiveness of this phrase by adding a few words. Now I tell them: *"I know you have many realtors to choose from, so I thank you for the opportunity to show you how I work."* Subliminally, I remind them that if there are so many realtors to choose from, they must have chosen me for a reason. Told, subliminally, that they have confidence in me, prospects come to believe it.

- Pacing and leading is a technique based on a proven idea that if the brain can verify two things as true, it will accept the reasonable third fact as being true also. So, if I tell a prospect

Selling Is Persuading

"My name is Jacob from Best Realty" the prospect's mind can quickly verify those two facts as true. Then, whatever is next such as *"the Woodbrook subdivision realtor"* rings true as well. Whatever your third piece of information is, it must be a reasonable fact. So, the subconscious will see Jacob as their subdivision's realtor.

- Use presuppositions (assumptions) to subliminally influence customers by constructing sentences that presuppose what you want your customers to do. For instance, you can ask *"Is there anything you find interesting in this house?"* or *"What do you find most interesting about this house?"* The first question assumes that there is almost nothing of interest, whereas the second one assumes there many interesting things to chose from. Instead of asking, *"Do you want to see the house?"* ask *"When do you want to see the house?"* Asking the question this way makes your customers think that they have already agreed to see the house. *"One of the things you would love about (this house) is..."* This phrase not only suggests that you will love what I am talking about, but that you will love other things too. *"As you consider the benefits of..."* This phrase contains the presupposition they are already doing it.

Chapter 11: Subliminal Persuasion

- Use of adverbs makes something seem trivial: obviously, naturally, clearly, of course... *Obviously, you need your family to be safe, and a house in this neighborhood will give you peace of mind. Of course, this house is expensive, but only the best is good enough.*

- People need to have some internal consistency, so they don't like to act against what they said. After showing a few houses we may restate what customers said they want, *"If I remember correctly, you said you wanted* a three bedrooms house, under $300,000 with a nice yard and close to schools and shopping. *I think we are in luck. Two of the houses we just looked at fit your criteria. So do you like this one or that one better?"* Most of the time, they will not even notice you emphasized their exact words, but they will feel uncomfortable to contradict their own words. It is tough to say "no" to what they said they wanted, and it is easier to say "yes." That is what subliminal persuasion is about.

- Use phases that are creating sense of safety, belonging, and importance.

    "What if..." This phrase removes ego from the discussion and creates a safe environment for exploring.

Selling Is Persuading

"Would it be helpful if…" This phrase shifts the focus from the problem to the solution.

"I need your help…" This phrase flips the roles of dominant and subordinate, engaging customers, and makes them feel important.

There are two techniques of subliminal persuasion—hidden commands and anchoring—that merit extra consideration.

Hidden Commands

A hidden command is a subliminal message embedded in another medium and designed to pass below the normal limits of perception. It is a short statement of no more than five words, which must include an action verb that implies thoughts, emotions, or actions. Research indicates that human brains are hard-wired to create mental images of verbs.

Here is a list of some action verbs: *Act, buy, change, decide, explore, finalize, get, heed, invest, know, listen, make, profit, reconsider, save, try, understand, visualize, work.*

Hidden commands communicate directly with the subconscious mind by hiding suggestions within spoken or written language. Said or written in a particular way, through the back door of the subconscious, they bypass conscious resistance. Subconscious mind is incapable of critical refusal of subliminal suggestion.

Here are examples of hidden commands.

Chapter 11: Subliminal Persuasion

- *Listen to me*   Usually home sellers **listen to me.**
- *Work with me*   You should **work with me,** so I can help you to **sell your house.**
- *Believe me*   It is not necessary to **believe me**; look at the statistics.
- *Trust me*   Don't just **trust me**, verify it.
- *Decide now*   If you don't **decide now**, there is no guarantee it will be there tomorrow.
- *Take action*   To buy a house, you have to **take action**.
- *Approve it*   **Approve it** and you are a proud homeowner.

Once you have created a set of hidden commands, prepare opening phrases to introduce them.

When you…, As you…, If you were to…, It is not necessary…, As you become aware…, Have you noticed…

As you **listen to me**, it is not necessary to **do what I say**.

Hidden commands intend to guide customers to think the way we would like them to think and to take the desired actions. They reduce resistance and make customers come to faster decisions. They motivate them to act. The information

Selling Is Persuading

conveyed by hidden commands is stored in the brain and affects the way people think, decide, and act. When we use these commands, we plant ideas into the subconscious mind. Nurturing them, we help them grow into actions.

By carefully constructing sentences that logically and contextually fit, and setting hidden commands apart with a tonality or font that spells out what we want customers to do, we can talk directly to the subconscious.

Learn how to make up commands appropriate to your business and to articulate them for maximum effect. Pause before a hidden command and say it louder. Pause after the command.

- "When you (pause) **hire us to sell your house, Michael,** (pause) all the work we do is to (pause) **get results now** (pause)."

- The prospect's subconscious mind will hear, **"hire us to sell your house, Michael… get results now."**

- "Unless you (pause) **listen to me**, you won't (pause) **list your house with me** (pause), which means you won't (pause) **have what you wish** (pause).

- Subconscious will hear, **"listen to me, list your house with me, and have what you wish."**

- Usually homeowners (pause) **do as I say.**

Chapter 11: Subliminal Persuasion

The following examples exploit the fact that the subconscious mind only functions in positive thoughts, never negative. It disregards the negative portion of a message, and registers only the positive part as a command.

- I wouldn't tell you to **buy this house**, that's your decision.
- I don't know if **signing up now is what you want to do**.
- I don't know if **deciding now is necessary** so you don't lose it.
- Don't believe that **my company is the best in the industry;** verify.
- I don't know if deciding to **buy this house today** will make you feel better.

Using hidden commands is not likely to persuade someone to buy something they are not interested in. But if they are talking to a salesperson about buying, for example, a new house, hidden commands can help them come to faster decisions and encourage them, sooner rather than later, to commit themselves.

One command will not translate into action. We have to repeat these commands strategically throughout the presentation. Making up commands we are comfortable with and putting them into our presentation, with practice we will do it subconsciously.

Many subliminal experts will tell you that just using "by now" frequently as in *"By now (pause) you can see that this house is luxurious"* is subconsciously taken as "buy now." What difference would it make if **by this** time next year your children will be in that school?

Instead of *"see you"* say *"good bye."* At the end of the discussion, if people are still hesitant to make an offer, we may say, *"People who* buy a house immediately *see the benefits of ownership. Before you* decide to make an offer *think about what additional information you need.* Good bye."

Words like "by," "buy," and "bye" that sound similarly are effective in subliminal persuasion. Words with double meaning might double your earnings. To incorporate this method of persuasion into the sales routine, choose words with double meanings in advance and practice using them as if they are not intended to persuade. For example, the word "like" has two meanings.

You like me can see the benefits of living in this neighborhood.

I like you appreciate convenience of this location as to transportation.

Developing positive feelings about you in customer's subconscious mind with hidden messages will ensure they are upbeat about working with you.

Certain phrases and words are powerful in engaging the subconscious mind such as *"how it would feel, can you imagine, visualize,* or *remember."*

Chapter 11: Subliminal Persuasion

How it would feel if you lived in a **house you could be proud of.**

Imagine what you may change if you would **be the owner of that house.**

By asking customers to imagine something, we bypass the critical part of the brain that throws objections and we "sneak' into their subconscious through the back door of imagination.

Simply saying phrases containing hidden commands is no guarantee that customers will do what we want. How we say them—tonality, voice variation, and vocal pacing—matter too. Stress the words you want to emphasize with your voice. Vocal stress occurs when the tone of your voice conveys the meaning beyond the words themselves. There is a lot of truth in the saying, *"It's not what you say but how you say it."* The concept of hidden commands revolves around stressing certain parts of what you are saying. *"Mr. Customer, this will **work for you**,"* would not work for you unless you emphasize "***work for you***." Emphasize the command for subconscious attention. In writing, this is done by using *italics* or **bold** font. In a conversation, it can be done with different voice tones or gestures.

Let us look at the phrase "You want to make an offer."

- If we keep our voice constant, it is a neutral statement. It does not add to or subtract from our persuasive effort.

- If we high pitch the last two words, it sounds like a question. There are languages, Russian for example, where people indicate a question by intonation only. In English it does not sound confident and, therefore, subtracts from persuasion.
- If we say the last two words in a louder and deeper voice, it is a hidden commend.
- You want to **make an offer**.

"Think how happy will your children be to play in this big yard, just as the children of the characters of the story, when you, **Mr. and Mrs. Smith, buy this home**.*"* Emphasized *"Mr. and Mrs. Smith buy this home"* will subconsciously be perceived as a command to buy.

Use hidden commands often. This of itself is a hidden command.

Anchoring

Russian scientist Ivan Pavlov used bells to call dogs to the food. After repeating this many times, he discovered that even with no food, dogs would salivate from hearing the bell. He *anchored* the food to the ringing. This is often referred to as Stimulus-Response. Similarly, we can stimulate emotional states. With an anchor, we link physical stimuli with emotional states. Like a real anchor holds a ship firmly in place, so verbal and nonverbal cues can keep a customer in an emotional harbor where they feel comfortable.

Anchoring is a technique that captures feelings, memories, and emotions of certain events and later brings up and reproduces the exact emotional feeling with a trigger. It is a connection of something seen, heard, or touched with a specific trigger.

Anchors can be established in the visual, auditory, and kinesthetic representational systems. By observing customers for a while, we can discover unique gestures, facial expressions, or voice variation to use as anchors for a particular customer. With an anchor, we can subliminally change the customer's attitude by eliciting memories and emotions.

To make anchors work, follow the next steps:

- With visual people, we can anchor the good feeling with a broad smile, enthusiastic nod, or energetic finger pointing. When attempting a close, we can elicit the same feeling with the same smile, nod, or gesture.

- With auditory people, tapping a pen, snapping fingers, or speaking louder would anchor a good feeling.

- With kinesthetic people, touching them on the shoulder or the elbow would anchor the emotion.

Selling Is Persuading

Master persuaders have the power to communicate with customers' subconscious using different techniques. New skills are perceived, and new levels of persuasion become a part of our conscience and subconscious.

To gain a true understanding of persuasion, we must understand both the conscious and subconscious ways of how people make decisions by interacting.

Epilogue

We, humans, can change not only our minds, but influence the minds of others. The ancient Greeks knew a lot about a lot of things, and many of their ideas, including about persuasion, are as relevant today as they have always been. But not even Aristotle could have imagined what we have learned about human nature and human brain. The more we know about human psychology and how human brain works, the more tools for changing minds we can develop. Persuasion is not magic. It's designed to give us a slight advantage that can make a big difference. In life, like in sports, a winner is often just slightly ahead of the runner-up.

By now, I hope that the curiosity that motivated you to read this book has been, at least partially, satisfied. Consider whether your mind has been changed by what you have read. I encourage not only recall what you read in this book but also to summon up your own experiences to understand and use the power of persuasion.

Selling Is Persuading

To bring this book to a close I would like to review the practices you can follow for achieving specific results you want:

1. Connect with people.
2. Evaluate the people on their personality types, dominant senses, and needs.
3. Familiarize yourself with different persuasion techniques for different people.
4. Use appropriate tools and words.
5. Choose a strategy and corresponding tactics for every situation.
6. Negotiate when persuasion alone does not work.
7. Persuade mostly through the back door of the subconscious.

Remember, the intention of these practices is mastery of different approaches: learn, practice, and apply. Imagine the changes taking place in your life as you continue working on discovering, developing, and applying new things.

Before you close this book, take a moment to consider what you have discovered, what you can take away with you, and how you can integrate this knowledge and the power of persuasion into your daily routine and make use of it in your professional and personal life.

You shall never be without power of persuasion. Your success is as good as your ability to persuade people to help you. Persuasion skills will keep you and your business moving forward.

Recommended Reading

If the curiosity that motivated you to read this book hasn't been fully satisfied, there many books that explore each subject you've read about in this book in more depth:

- *How to Win Friends & Influence People* by Dale Carnegie
- *Please Understand Me II* by David Keirsey
- *The Psychology of Selling* by Brian Tracy
- *Influence: The Psychology of Persuasion* by Robert Cialdini
- *Yes! 50 Scientifically Proven Ways to Be More Persuasive* by Robert Cialdini, Noah Goldstein, and Steven Martin
- *The Elements of Persuasion: Use Storytelling to Pitch Better, Sell Faster & Win More Business* by Richard Maxwell and Robert Dickman
- *Need to Know Body Language* by C. Boyes
- *Exactly What to Say: The Magic Words for Influence and Impact* by Phil M. Jones

Acknowledgments

Many thanks go to people who made this book possible:

To Caren Niele for setting me off on this journey when the English language was still a mystery to me.

To Ora Avni for reading and editing the manuscript.

To Glen Lippman for his opinion and suggestions.

To Cliff Comanday and InkWell writer's group for their friendly critique and advice.

To Caryn DeVincenti, Regional Director Florida Writer's Association, for her guidance.

YAKOV GRINSHPUN'S twenty-five-year career as a physics teacher in the Soviet Union included a lot of convincing. Another quarter of a century as a successful realtor in the United States required even more persuasion skills. Realizing that they are the main ingredient of success, his focus has been on researching, developing, and applying a system that lets anyone to become a skillful persuader.

Yakov has been interviewed for Florida Realtor Magazine and achieved the highest ranking in the Toastmasters International.

He is an active member of the InkWell Writer's group and an avid member of the Intellectual Conversation Group.

For more persuasion tips, visit
sellingispersuading.wordpress.com

www.ingramcontent.com/pod-product-compliance
Lightning Source LLC
Chambersburg PA
CBHW021811170526
45157CB00007B/2546